The Great War in British Literature

Adria v

Series Editor: Adrian Barlow

UNIVERSITY PRESS

PUBLISHED BY THE PRESS SYNDICATE OF THE UNIVERSITY OF CAMBRIDGE
The Pitt Building, Trumpington Street, Cambridge, United Kingdom

CAMBRIDGE UNIVERSITY PRESS
The Edinburgh Building, Cambridge CB2 2RU, UK
40 West 20th Street, New York, NY 10011–4211, USA
477 Williamstown Road, Port Melbourne, VIC 3207, Australia
Ruiz de Alarcón 13, 28014 Madrid, Spain
Dock House, The Waterfront, Cape Town 8001, South Africa

http://www.cambridge.org

First published 2000
Third printing 2002

Printed in the United Kingdom at the University Press, Cambridge

Typefaces: Clearface and Mixage   *System:* QuarkXPress® 4.04

A catalogue record for this book is available from the British Library

ISBN 0 521 64420 8 paperback

Prepared for publication by Gill Stacey
Designed by Tattersall Hammarling & Silk
Cover illustration: *The Return to the Front: Victoria Railway Station, 1916* by
Richard Jack, courtesy of York City Art Gallery. Presented by the artist, 1928.

Contents

The Great War: some key dates and battles of the Western Front

1914

4 August	Britain declares war against Germany
23 August	British Expeditionary Force (BEF) in retreat from Mons
September	Battle of the Marne
October – November	First Battle of Ypres

1915

March	Neuve Chapelle
April	Gallipoli landings; Second Battle of Ypres (gas used by German troops for first time)
May	Sinking of the Lusitania
September	Battle of Loos (gas used by British army for first time)
December	Retreat from Gallipoli

1916

January	Conscription introduced
February	Siege of Verdun launched
May	Naval Battle of Jutland
1 July	Somme offensive begins
September	Tanks used for first time
November	Stalemate ends Battle of Somme

1917

April	Battle of Arras; capture of Vimy Ridge
April	USA declares war on Germany
July	Third Battle of Ypres; Passchendaele
November	Battle of Cambrai; Russian Revolution

1918

March–July	German offensives: Picardy – Aisne – Marne
18 July	Allied counter-offensive launched
8 August	Battle of Amiens begins
15 August	British troops cross the Ancre
30 August	British troops cross the Somme
29 September	British and Empire forces begin attack on Hindenberg Line
9 November	Kaiser Wilhelm II of Germany abdicates
11 November	Armistice between the Allies and Germany

1919

28 June	Signing of the Treaty of Versailles

Introduction

The Great War of 1914–18 continues to fascinate readers and writers. This book aims to explore the different ways in which the Great War has featured both as a genre and as a theme in British literature of the past century; it asks what actually is the literature of the Great War, and looks at different ways in which people have read this literature, reacted to it and used it.

For the past eighty years people throughout the world have remembered the Great War. Partly the sheer scale of the casualties meant that more British, French, Belgian, German families than in any previous conflict lost sons, husbands, fathers – or knew families who had – and so there was private grief and remembrance on an unprecedented scale. In Britain, there has also been the institution of the annual Remembrance Day, an act of collective remembering, usually centred on the local war memorial – still a focal point in most cities, towns and villages:

> They shall not grow old, as we that are left grow old.
> Age shall not weary them, nor the years condemn.
> At the going down of the sun, and in the morning,
> We will remember them.

These lines, written as early as 1914 in a poem by Laurence Binyon, are part of the Act of Remembrance, the national ritual that involves a two-minute silence at 11 o'clock on the Sunday closest to 11 November, the eleventh hour of the eleventh day of the eleventh month – the moment of the original 1918 armistice. The Act of Remembrance is one of the very few rituals that still cuts across religion, race and class in Britain: Binyon's poem recognises only two classes – the dead and the survivors.

Right from the start of the war, this polarity between the living and the dead underpinned the dialogue between writers and their audience. Rupert Brooke's poem 'The Soldier' is one of the most famous and (by some) one of the most derided poems of the century – though its survival, and the survival of interest in Brooke as a person, suggests it has a literary robustness that has often been undervalued. It is accused of naiveté and – worse still – of being a 'ridiculous pastoral' ('some corner of a foreign field / That is forever England'). And yet, as a poem it is far from being a straightforward piece of sentimental patriotic verse.

Look how it actually begins:

> If I should die, think only this of me …

The speaker is addressing a listener, who is told to 'think', meaning here, 'use your imagination to remember me in this way'. Who is this listener? A girl friend, a mother, a fellow soldier? The poem is not, in one sense, concerned with the speaker's own feelings for and about England so much as with how the listener – whoever he or she is – might be able to come to terms with his death, if and when it occurs. The instruction 'think' is repeated at the start of line 9 of the sonnet ('And think, this heart, all evil shed away ...'); again, it means 'imagine that ...'. To remember him, if he dies, in these nostalgically English terms may – the poem implies – help to make sense of his death. With the war only starting, the poem looks forward to the need people will have for remembrance when it is over. Read in this way, the patriotic imagery ('A body of England's, breathing English air', etc.) is not flag-waving by the speaker, but a set of reference points offered to the listener. Brooke's 'The Soldier' is in fact one of the earliest examples of Great War writing that is, in essence, a dialogue between the living (the survivors) and the dead or (in Brooke's case) the soon-to-be-dead.

This book deals only with British writing – that is, writing about the Great War in English by writers from the United Kingdom. Inevitably, then, it will be a partial treatment of the Great War in literature: writers, critics and cultural historians today stress that to understand fully the nature of war poetry, for instance, it is important to compare and contrast the poetry of German, French and other writers. One of the most celebrated and influential novels about the Great War is *All Quiet on the Western Front* by Erich Maria Remarque, who fought for Germany against the French. His book has been twice filmed, once in America and more recently in England. In translation it has been read and studied in British schools more than perhaps any English book on the Great War, except for Siegfried Sassoon's *Memoirs of an Infantry Officer*. Part 6 of this book features a chronology and reading list with pointers to books dealing with the Great War written by, and about, writers outside the United Kingdom.

In part, reasons of space dictate that this book's scope will be limited to British writing. But there is an important sense in which the Great War in British literature is a different subject from, say, the Great War in French, American or German literature. The Great War challenged, and then helped to redefine, the different ideas of Englishness which have been a major preoccupation of writers throughout the 20th century. The sheer survival of the Great War in modern memory (to adapt the title of one of the most important books on the subject: *The Great War and Modern Memory* by Paul Fussell) is more evident in British culture – television and film, as well as literature – than in other countries, and suggests that this process is still going on. Through its introduction to the literary, cultural and critical study of British writing from and about the Great War, this book invites readers to consider how and why this subject remains as important at the start of the 21st century as it was throughout the 20th.

How this book is organised

Part 1: Reading the Great War
Part 1 is a survey of British writing concerned with, and deriving from, the Great War throughout the 20th century.

Part 2: Approaching the texts
Part 2 examines the different types of writing that go to make up the literature of the Great War.

Part 3: Texts and extracts
Part 3 contains texts and extracts discussed in the rest of the book, or used as the focus for tasks and assignments. Most of the material in this section is not easily accessible elsewhere; poems already easily found in anthologies of war poetry and extracts from familiar novels still in print have not been included.

Part 4: Critical approaches
This part explores the different ways in which critics and readers have reacted to the literature of the Great War.

Part 5: How to write about the Great War in British literature
Part 5 offers guidelines and assignments for those for whom this book is chiefly intended: students covering the topic as part of an advanced course in literary studies.

Part 6: Resources
This part contains a chronology of texts and writers discussed in the book, together with guidance on further reading, and a glossary and index. (Terms which appear in the glossary are highlighted in bold type throughout the book.)

At different points throughout the book, and at the end of Parts 1, 2, 4 and 5 there are tasks and assignments, designed to help the reader reflect on ideas discussed in the text. Where reference to a poem or prose extract is followed by a page reference, the passage will be found in this book, usually in Part 3: Texts and extracts.

1 | Reading the Great War

- What is the relationship between literature and war?

- How did attitudes and values before 1914 shape the writing of the Great War?

- What impact did the development of the war have on the way people wrote about it?

- How did writing about the war evolve after the fighting was over?

Writing about war before 1914

Although the fighting ended with the Armistice (11 November 1918), politically, the Great War only ended the following year with the signing of the Treaty of Versailles. Many war memorials therefore give 1914–19 as the start and end of what was one of the defining events of the 20th century. It began (for most people in Britain) very unexpectedly during a sweltering hot summer, and ended countless deaths later after much of northern France and Belgium had been reduced to a wasteland.

This uncertainty about when the Great War really ended is significant because in a sense the aftermath of the war still affects us today: we have not put it behind us; we keep returning to it. The Edwardian era which was abruptly brought to a close by the war seems as remote to us at the start of the 21st century as no doubt the Napoleonic Wars and the Battle of Waterloo (1815) did to those about to be caught up in the events of 1914. One of the most famous English novels set in the Edwardian era, L.P. Hartley's *The Go-Between* (1953), famously begins: 'The past is a foreign country: they do things differently there.' Yet novels are still being written which make the Great War seem very familiar territory, and most school students in Britain know more about the poetry of the First World War than they do about the poetry of any other period – including their own. The Great War, as we encounter it through literature, is both present and past. The voices we listen to sound like voices from our own time, not from an earlier one.

Literary historians and teachers like to label periods with particular names – Victorian, Edwardian and so on – and then fit writers into these periods. So Tennyson (1809–92) slots neatly into the Victorian period. His poem 'The Charge of the Light Brigade', about a disastrous incident that occurred in the Crimean War (1854), seems to epitomise Victorian values. It celebrates devotion to duty, heroism in the face of certain death – the glamour of chivalry:

Their's not to reason why,
Their's but to do and die:
Into the valley of Death
  Rode the six hundred.

The words here present no apparent difficulties, but the tone of the poem ('Honour the Light Brigade! Oh, the wild charge they made!') is no longer one most people are comfortable with when discussing death in battle – and the writing of the Great War has largely been responsible for this shift.

The South Africa War of 1899–1902 was for most Victorians their first experience of a major war, albeit one fought in another continent and a different hemisphere. Boer War memorials were erected, bearing the names of individual combatants who had died – ordinary soldiers and officers side-by-side. These civic memorials reflected the fact that for the first time in living memory large numbers of English, Welsh and Scots had died fighting for their country. These numbers were later to seem tiny compared with those of 1914–18, but the impact was significant as a preparation for the Great War. In terms of literature, however, the abiding poetic statement from this era is one which provokes a very ambiguous reaction:

The sand of the desert is sodden red, –
  Red with the wreck of a square that broke; –
The Gatling's jammed and the Colonel dead,
  And the regiment blind with dust and smoke.
The river of death has brimmed his banks,
  And England's far, and Honour a name,
But the voice of a schoolboy rallies the ranks:
  'Play up! play up! and play the game!'

               (Henry Newbolt 'Vitai Lampada')

This writing sets out to present the actuality of war ('The Gatling's jammed and the Colonel dead') while invoking the same qualities that Tennyson's poem was thought to celebrate; however, a line such as 'The river of death has brimmed his banks' sounds today like a substitute for real thought or description, while the idea that a mere schoolboy second lieutenant could rally 'the ranks' (i.e. the 'other ranks', not his fellow officers) by appealing to their sense of war as a game of cricket seems remote and faintly ridiculous to us. The point is, though, that it did not seem ridiculous to those who read it first nor, indeed, to those who went on reading it during the First World War and for many years afterwards. This Victorian public school idealism affirmed a vision of service, loyalty and sacrifice which was important to those who survived the war and had to make sense of the enormous death toll at the end of it.

A writer like Thomas Hardy (1840–1928), on the other hand, straddles the 19th and 20th centuries. By and large, his novels belong to the former and his best-known poetry to the latter. His attitude to war seems also to straddle the two centuries: he doesn't find glamour in war, but he manages to view it with a certain detachment. His 1915 poem 'In Time of "The Breaking of Nations"' sees the First World War – even while it is going on – as rather trivial compared with the fundamentals of ordinary human life:

> Yonder a maid and her wight
>   Come whispering by:
> War's annals will cloud into night
>   Ere their story die.

The sense of timelessness here is reinforced by the use of old-fashioned words such as 'yonder' and 'wight' (meaning 'man'). Archaic **diction** in poetry – the use of a particular kind of old-fashioned vocabulary – was still conventional and indeed expected by most readers long after the end of the 19th century; and when Hardy introduces more informal diction into his writing it leaves a reader of nearly a century later rather confused:

> In our heart of hearts believing
>   Victory crowns the just,
>   And that braggarts must
>   Surely bite the dust,
> Press we to the field ungrieving,
> In our heart of hearts believing
>   Victory crowns the just.

('Men Who March Away')

This poem, written in the opening days of the war, sets out to express the feelings of soldiers cheerfully enlisting in a war that was supposed to be over by Christmas. To us the language of 'braggarts must Surely bite the dust' sounds quaint and naive. It certainly does not sound like the authentic voice of a real army.

Neither Newbolt nor Hardy fought in the war, but it was their poetry which had been read by, and taught at school to, the generation of young men destined to be the casualties or survivors of the Western Front.

The novel 1910–14

At the outbreak of the war, a number of young writers were beginning to establish reputations and to be widely read, and the period of 1912–14 was one of considerable excitement in the arts generally – although this excitement was largely confined to those with a taste for the avant-garde and for new developments in music, art, architecture and literature. In Europe the music of Stravinsky and the paintings of Picasso seemed to signal a break, not just an evolution, from the past. Out of America came jazz; and ragtime entertainments began to replace the music hall entertainments of the Victorian and Edwardian popular theatre as the stage shows to be seen. A new generation of novelists was beginning to emerge, challenging the orthodoxies of writers such as Arnold Bennett (1867–1931) and John Galsworthy (1867–1933).

Pre-war issues: continuity and identity

Galsworthy's sequence of novels, *The Forsyte Saga*, (only half completed by 1914) seemed to leave the surface of middle-class, metropolitan London unscratched even if the relationships of the individual characters endured various strains and traumas. By contrast, the novel *Howards End* (1910) by E.M. Forster (1879–1970) explored the insecurities of middle-class England by creating two families, the Schlegels and the Wilcoxes, whose lives clash in a series of encounters – commercial, cultural and sexual – but are finally reconciled when the Wilcoxes' world of 'telegrams and anger' is shown to be less resilient than the world represented by Howards End itself. The survival of this old house on the edge of suburbia suggests for Forster a deep sense of the continuity of England and of the importance of personal relationships at a time when such things are under threat. In the novel, London is in a state of flux as the city expands and old houses (including the Schlegels') are demolished to make way for new blocks of flats. Ugliness and commerce threaten culture and continuity. The orphaned Schlegel sisters, Helen and Margaret, had a German father and English mother: their English aunt, Mrs Munt, insists they are 'English to the backbone' and Forster himself notes that they are not, as he ironically puts it, 'Germans of the dreadful sort'. The whole novel in fact argues that stereotypes and prejudices are dangerous: 'the remark "England and Germany are bound to fight" renders war a little more likely every time that it is made, and is therefore made the more readily by the gutter press of either nation'.

For Forster, personal relations, culture, landscape and a profound sense of the importance of place are the things worth preserving. For another novelist making his reputation just before the outbreak of the war, D.H. Lawrence (1885–1930), the same priorities apply, but a novel such as *Sons and Lovers* approaches them from a different perspective. For Lawrence, landscape is disfigured by industrialisation and the same process diminishes the lives of the people who struggle to survive in the mining towns that blight the Nottinghamshire and Derbyshire landscape where Lawrence himself grew up. Paul Morel, the central character of *Sons and Lovers*, refuses to become a miner; instead he tries to make a reputation for himself as an artist; Will Brangwen in *The Rainbow* (which Lawrence began to write in 1913, the year *Sons and Lovers* was published) becomes a wood carver; and in *Women in Love*, written during the war itself, one of Will's daughters, Gudrun, becomes a painter. As with Lawrence, so with his characters: as their cultural horizons expand, they move away from Nottinghamshire to London and abroad – to Germany and Italy. Will Brangwen's mother is a Polish widow, Gudrun has as lovers first the son of a local mine owner, then a German artist. (Lawrence had himself eloped with and then married a German woman from an aristocratic family.)

But for Lawrence no less than Forster, the continuity of the English landscape remains a potent symbol. At the start of *The Rainbow*, the Brangwens have been farming for generations in the Erewash valley outside Nottingham, and this landscape – almost their private territory – is violated by the coming of industry. But, just as Forster's Schlegels rely on the world of finance and business to supply the private income that enables them to enjoy the cultured life they lead, so Lawrence's Brangwens come to depend on local industry: 'The town grew rapidly, the Brangwens were kept busy producing supplies, they became richer, they were almost tradesmen.'

Pre-war issues: the role of women

Another thing that both Forster and Lawrence have in common in their novels is a preoccupation with the emancipation of women, not primarily in terms of the Vote and the Suffragette movement, but in terms of their opportunities for self-development in the modern world. While the older generation of women in their novels accept their roles within the family, the younger seek a new role and a new voice for themselves. Thus Helen Schlegel, at the close of *Howards End*, has become a single mother with no intention of marrying for the sake of propriety. Ursula Brangwen, at the close of *The Rainbow*, has miscarried a child conceived during a failed relationship, and now looks forward to a world in which women would have a different role.

The idea of England, the importance of landscape and the earth, the mechanised, industrial world and the role of women – these, then, were some of the preoccupations of writers and readers at the start of the war, and to a large extent they continued to shape, and be reflected by, the writing that came out of the war itself.

Poetry 1910–14

The Georgians

In poetry, these tensions were evident by 1914 in the different groups of young poets who were beginning to establish reputations for themselves. On the one hand were the Georgians, contributors to a new anthology called *Georgian Poetry*. (This title reflected the belief of the editor, Eddie Marsh, that the new reign – George V had succeeded Edward VII in 1910 – meant a new start for English poetry.) Broadly, the Georgian poets saw their job as being to make poetry accessible to a wide audience, to celebrate ordinary – particularly rural and suburban – life rather than grand poetic themes and to do so in a diction that was neither clichéd nor grandiose. These aspirations may sound very limited today, but they had a strong appeal at the time, and the five *Georgian Poetry* anthologies which appeared between 1912 and 1922 were immensely popular. They helped to create a new readership for poetry in the years immediately before the war and gave Rupert Brooke an audience for his sonnet sequence '1914'. Other war poets – Siegfried Sassoon, Edmund Blunden among them – were later to be labelled Georgians, and Wilfred Owen wrote home ecstatically to his mother, 'I am held peer by the Georgians' even though his poems did not actually feature in the anthologies.

Another poet who was close to the Georgians without ever actually being published in the *Georgian Poetry* anthologies was Edward Thomas, who had already established a strong reputation as a perceptive critic of the contemporary poetry scene. Up to 1914 Thomas had published a good deal of prose, particularly about the English and Welsh countryside. When, as the war began, he started to write poetry with the encouragement of his friend, the American poet Robert Frost, his writing showed the Georgian style at its most effective:

A Private
This ploughman dead in battle slept out of doors
Many a frozen night, and merrily
Answered staid drinkers, good bedmen, and all bores:
'At Mrs. Greenland's Hawthorn Bush,' said he,
'I slept.' None knew which bush. Above the town,
Beyond 'The Drover,' a hundred spot the down
In Wiltshire. And where now he last he sleeps
More sound in France – that, too, he secret keeps.

▶ In what sense, if at all, can 'A Private' be called a war poem? How far does it differ from other war poems you have encountered? What do you think is the point of the poem?

The Imagists

Much less popular at the time than the Georgian poets (but in retrospect highly significant for the development of **modernism** in English poetry) were the Imagists. This group of poets was 'led' by the American writer Ezra Pound, who in 1912 published an anthology called *Des Imagistes* to promote his own poetry and that of writers such as Richard Aldington and Hilda Doolittle (whose work always appeared under her initials H.D.). **Imagism**, the name for the style of writing which appeared in the Imagist anthologies, took a more radical view of poetry than that of the Georgian poets, experimenting with free verse forms which took poetry much further from Victorian and Edwardian conventions than the Georgians were prepared to go. Whereas the Georgians were happy to deploy conventional verse forms – the sonnet, blank verse, **lyric** quatrains or (as in Thomas's poem above) rhyming couplets – the Imagists largely abandoned rhyme and iambic metre in favour of *vers libre*.

Richard Aldington, both as a poet and as a novelist, was to become one of the most important writers to fight in – and survive – the trenches, and his poetry reflects two tensions: between remaining a poet while being a soldier at the same time, and between the stylistic features which set the Imagists apart from the Georgians:

> *Picket*
> Dusk and deep silence ...
>
> Three soldiers huddled on a bench
> Over a red-hot brazier,
> And a fourth who stands apart
> Watching the cold rainy dawn.
>
> Then the familiar sound of birds –
> Clear cock-crow, caw of rooks,
> Frail pipe of the linnet, the 'ting! ting!' of chaffinches,
> And over all the lark
> Outpiercing even the robin ...
>
> Wearily the sentry moves
> Muttering the one word: 'Peace'.

The Imagists took over a feminist magazine, the *New Freewoman*, and turned it into their own literary journal, *The Egoist*, which Aldington edited. The principles of Imagism, as originally set out by Ezra Pound and the poet F.S. Flint, offered a clear statement of what an Imagist poem should and should not contain:

1   Direct treatment of the 'thing', whether subjective or objective.
2   To use absolutely no word that does not contribute to
    presentation.
3   As regards rhythm: to compose in sequence of the musical
    phrase, not in sequence of the metronome.

Aldington was editor of *The Egoist* until he joined the Army in 1916; he was
succeeded by T.S. Eliot (1888–1965) who, though not a member of the Imagist
group, was much closer to them than to the Georgians. In fact, however, it is
important not to over-emphasise the differences between Georgians and the
modernists – Pound, the Imagists and T.S. Eliot: at first, there was a good deal of
overlapping between them, and writers such as D.H. Lawrence had poems
published in both Georgian and Imagist publications.

▶ How well does Aldington's poem 'Picket' illustrate the Imagist principles?
Compare the poem with Isaac Rosenberg's poem 'Returning, We Hear the Larks'
(page 90). What do they have in common, and how do they differ, both in their
themes and in their forms? Can you tell that one is written by a 'Georgian' poet and
the other by an 'Imagist'?

Georgians and modernists

Later, as the optimism of the period 1912–14 was abruptly killed off by the war,
Georgian poetry came to seem narrow and timid in scope. Its continuing appeal to
a mainly middle-class conservative audience made it seem less relevant to a
changed readership. The challenge of modernist poems such as T.S. Eliot's *The
Waste Land* (1922) seemed more rewarding and more in keeping with the post-war
mood of anxiety and uncertainty.

The Waste Land is all the things that Georgian Poetry is not: it is complex,
elusive in its meaning and allusive in its references; its central locations are the
city, not the country; it does not offer a pastoral vision of a renewed England but
an unromantic panorama of urban decay and despair. The fact that it has become
one of the central poems of the 20th century and T.S. Eliot one of the century's
most important poets has also done much to overshadow the contribution made
by the Georgians to the evolution of poetry since 1900. Yet Georgian Poetry is
still important for providing the context within which most of the war poets –
Siegfried Sassoon, Edmund Blunden and Isaac Rosenberg in particular –
established themselves.

'England' and 'Englishness'

It wasn't surprising that the modernists should have had less interest than the Georgians in the idea of England and Englishness: Pound, H.D. and Eliot were Americans living in London, and their inspiration at first came as much from European as from English literature. A writer like Richard Aldington, though English, was also more influenced in his early career by what was happening in metropolitan London and in France and America. For the Georgians, however, the physical importance of England was not just an ideal: in the summer of 1914 several of them (Lascelles Abercrombie and Wilfred Gibson, together with Robert Frost and, intermittently, the playwright John Drinkwater, Edward Thomas and Rupert Brooke) were based in a remote village called Dymock on the Gloucestershire–Herefordshire border. Here the poets and their families lived in rented farm cottages; Frost later said – only half jokingly – that he had wanted to know what it was like to live under thatch. Here, too, they wrote and published a magazine called *New Numbers*, which helped to keep their work in the public eye between the first and second volumes of *Georgian Poetry*.

Living so close to the land during a golden summer in a rural area, it was not surprising that the poetry the **Dymock poets** wrote just as the war was about to break should have evoked an idyllic, pastoral ideal of England. It should be added that this was essentially a vision of southern England: from a literary perspective England north of D.H. Lawrence's Nottinghamshire hardly existed in the writing of 1914. The sense that not just the landscape but the actual soil of England embodied everything for which Englishmen were prepared to fight may seem sentimental today, but at the start of the war it provided a potent symbol. When Edward Thomas was asked why he was prepared to join up and fight, he bent down, picked up a clod of soil, held it out and said, 'Literally, for this.' Rupert Brooke, in an essay published in 1914, described the feelings of 'An Unusual Young Man' (in reality, Brooke himself) on hearing the news that war had been declared:

> His astonishment grew as the full flood of 'England' swept him on from thought to thought. He felt the triumphant helplessness of a lover. Grey, uneven little fields, and small ancient hedges rushed before him, wild flowers, elms and beeches, gentleness, sedate houses of red brick, proudly unassuming, a countryside of rambling hills and friendly copses. He seemed to be raised high, looking down on a landscape compounded of the western view from the Cotswolds, and the Weald, and the high land in Wiltshire, and the Midlands seen from the hills above Prince's Risborough. And all this to the accompaniment of tunes heard long ago, an intolerable number of them being hymns.
>
> (from *Letters from America*)

For Brooke, the news of the war offered a kind of epiphany, a quasi-mystical revelation ('He seemed to be raised high') of the 'English heaven' about which he speaks at the end of 'The Soldier'. Meanwhile Edward Thomas, who had probably walked more miles over southern England and Wales than anyone else of his generation, was experiencing a rather different epiphany:

> Now all roads lead to France
> And heavy is the tread
> Of the living; but the dead
> Returning lightly dance ...

('Roads')

▶ Read again Rupert Brooke's sonnet 'The Soldier', and the discussion of it on pages 7–8. Now read the following comments on the poem by Christopher Hassall, who wrote one of the first full biographies of Brooke:

> The 'soldier' was meant by Brooke to be still a civilian, someone who had discovered a way of bequeathing his possessions, his country to the earth (which in a way would *become* his country) and the rest, the sights and sounds, would somehow be returned whence they came, for others to enjoy ... The poetical manner is candid like the author's face. Not only has the Anglo-American tradition that was to follow in English verse [i.e. the modernism of Pound and Eliot] made the simple rhetoric outmoded, but the attitude of mind itself, the unquestioning acceptance of a state of affairs, has become suspect. To many it must seem as naive as saying the Apostles Creed and meaning what one says. Brooke wrote straight from the shoulder, as it were, without what the fashionable modern would regard as the saving grace of a qualifying remark. And yet therein lies the strength. He had not only arrived at a faith but at mastery of the traditional style.

▶ Do you find this view of Brooke and of his most famous poem convincing? What do you learn from this passage about a traditionalist's view of modernism?

▶ Read the other poems in the *1914* sonnet sequence. Do you find them more or less appealing than 'The Soldier'?

Poetry and the war 1914–16

It is hard to imagine that poetry will ever play such a role again as it did in the Great War. In the first two years of the war (until the catastrophic Battle of the Somme) this role was closely linked to the patriotic enthusiasm which led so many men to join up. The death of Rupert Brooke in 1915 prompted an obituary article in *The Times* written by Winston Churchill who called Brooke a 'poet-soldier' and thus helped both to create the idea both of a war poet and of the amateur soldier who was first and foremost a writer; 'The Soldier' was read from the pulpit of St Paul's Cathedral as part of a patriotic sermon. The American novelist Henry James, in the Introduction to Brooke's posthumously published *Letters from America* (1916), acknowledged that Brooke had already become a legend:

> Rupert Brooke, young, happy, radiant, extraordinarily endowed and irresistibly attaching, virtually met a soldier's death, met it in the stress of action and the all but immediate presence of the enemy …
> With twenty reasons fixing the interest and the charm that will henceforth abide in his name and constitute, as we may say, his legend … Rupert expressed us all, at the highest tide of our actuality …

(In fact Brooke died of blood poisoning while on a troop ship bound for Gallipoli.)

When even Henry James could launch into such eulogy, it is not hard to understand how easily Brooke's death and poetry were exploited to raise morale and help recruitment at home. But Brooke was not the only poet writing in 1914: in the first two years of the war a great deal of poetry was written and published – not all of it straightforward recruiting propaganda. In 'All the Hills and Vales Along' Charles Hamilton Sorley gave the marching song an ironic twist:

> All the hills and vales along
> Earth is bursting into song,
> And the singers are the chaps
> Who are going to die perhaps.

The opening note of optimism in calling the soldiers 'singers' is immediately undercut by describing them as 'the chaps Who are going to die perhaps'. The second half of the stanza adds to the ambivalent tone:

> O sing, marching men,
> Till the valleys ring again.
> Give your gladness to earth's keeping,
> So be glad, when you are sleeping.

'Sleeping' here, as nearly always in war poetry, has undertones of death, and the implicit suggestion that death is the most desirable – or at least the inevitable – end for the soldier is made explicit in the last stanza of the poem:

> On, marching men, on
> To the gates of death with song.
> Sow your gladness for earth's reaping,
> So you may be glad, though sleeping.
> Strew your gladness on earth's bed,
> So be merry, so be dead.

Sorley (like another of the war poets, Edmund Blunden) went almost straight from public school into the trenches. He was travelling in Germany when the war broke out, came back to England and enlisted, was commissioned, sent to France and died during the Battle of Loos in October 1915, aged twenty. His poem seems to celebrate the chance of fighting ('Sow your gladness for earth's reaping' – notice how the earth is personified here to harvest the future happiness planted by the soldiers) with an almost Tennysonian enthusiasm: 'to the Gates of Death with song'. But this apparent note of patriotic sacrifice – the cheerful willingness to die for one's country, confident that this will ensure a peaceful future – is abruptly offset by the final line, 'So be merry, so be dead.' This is a more sober view of death than that expressed by Rupert Brooke in 'The Soldier' but it is perhaps closer to Brooke's famous comment 'Well, if Armageddon's on, I suppose one should be there.' (from *Letters from America*)

In the poetry of Edward Thomas, who was over the age of conscription and who could have remained a civilian throughout the war, a mixture of conflicting personal anxieties about whether or not to fight can be found. 'As The Team's Head Brass' presents a conversation between an elder ploughman, working alone because his work-mate has been killed in France, and a speaker uncertain whether or not to enlist:

> 'Have you been out?' 'No.' 'And don't want to, perhaps?'
> 'If I could only come back again, I should.
> I could spare an arm. I shouldn't want to lose
> A leg. If I should lose my head, why, so,
> I should want nothing more ...'

Elsewhere, in 'This Is No Case of Petty Right or Wrong', Thomas insisted that the motives for fighting had to be clearly distinguished from general anti-German propaganda:

I hate not Germans, nor grow hot
With love of Englishmen, to please newspapers.
Beside my hate for one fat patriot
My hatred of the Kaiser is love true: –
A kind of god he is, banging a drum.

The 'one fat patriot' here was Thomas's own father. At the end of this poem, however, Thomas resolves his dilemma by concluding:

... with the best and meanest Englishmen
I am one in crying, God save England, lest
We lose what never slaves and cattle blessed.
The ages made her that made us from the dust:
She is all we know and live by, and we trust
She is good and must endure, loving her so:
And as we love ourselves we hate her foe.

Once in uniform, the poets of the Great War had to come to terms with a new existence. Each responded in his own way and coped with experiences that depended on their rank and circumstances. When the poet Edmund Blunden came to introduce a revised edition of his book *Undertones of War* (1928) he said:

This book, which was written with no grander ambition than to preserve some of a multitude of impressions, and admirations, is a sketch of a happy battalion – happy in spite of terrible tasks and daily destruction. I have been blamed for casting a romantic light on such a damnable subject as real war. But I did no more than put on paper what most of my companions felt too.

On the other hand, Edward Thomas, in a poem ironically called 'Home', wrote plaintively:

If I should ever more admit
Than the mere word I could not endure it
For a day longer: this captivity
Must somehow come to an end, else I should be
Another man, as often now I seem,
Or this life be only an evil dream.

No one expressed the two senses of home (both England as a concept – the embodiment of what one was fighting for – and the specific longing to be back in the English countryside) more movingly than Ivor Gurney (1890–1937). Gurney lived in Gloucestershire, close enough to the able to cycle to visit the Dymock poets whose work he much admired. His poetry is written with an understated irony which just manages to control an overwhelming sense of horror at the necessary actions of war:

To England – A Note

I watched the boys of England where they went
Through mud and water to do appointed things,
See one a stake, and one wire-netting brings,
And one comes slowly under a burden bent
Of ammunition. Though the strength be spent
They "carry on" under the shadowing wings
Of Death the ever-present. And hark, one sings
Although no joy from the grey skies be lent.

Are these the heroes – these? have kept from you
The power of primal savagery so long?
Shall break the devil's legions? These they are
Who do in silence what they might boast to do;
In the height of battle tell the world in song
How they do hate and fear the face of War.

In this sonnet, every phrase that might seem to imply a conventional patriotic or propaganda response is undercut: 'the boys of England' focuses on the fact that the soldiers are no more than boys – often almost literally – and phrases such as 'the power of primal savagery' become mere rhetoric when set alongside the stark understatement of 'to do appointed things' and 'They "carry on"'. Gurney's 'Note' to England is a warning note: the soldiers of whom he writes are heroes, they are entitled to boast about what they are doing on England's behalf. But what drives them on in battle is not hatred of 'the devil's legions' but hatred of war itself.

This poem, published in 1917, expresses publicly the sense that war is literally unspeakable (the soldiers 'do in silence' the things they have to do) and not a subject for unthinking propaganda.

To be both a poet and a soldier thus imposed particular strains, which were not always kept beneath the surface: Isaac Rosenberg (see Part 3, pages 90–91) expressed in letters the suffering he felt, but managed to achieve an impersonality in his poems which gives them extraordinary power and poignancy. Writing to Lascelles Abercrombie (one of the Dymock poets, who was never able to enlist because of poor eyesight) he exclaimed, 'Believe me, the army is the most detestable invention on this earth and nobody but a private in the army knows what it is to be a slave.' On the other hand, in a letter to the poet Laurence Binyon (author of 'For the Fallen', see page 7) he could write:

> I am determined that this war, with all its powers for devastation, shall not master my poeting; that is, if I am lucky enough to come through all right. I will not leave a corner of my consciousness covered up, but saturate myself with the strange and extraordinary new conditions of this life, and it will all refine itself into poetry later on.

▶ Compare Isaac Rosenberg's letters (page 91) and his poems, 'Returning, We Hear the Larks' (page 90) and 'Dead Man's Dump'. In what ways does he manage to refine 'the strange and extraordinary conditions of this life' into poetry here?

The difficulty of being both soldier and poet is succinctly expressed by David Jones (1895–1974) in the Preface to his account of the war, *In Parenthesis*: 'We find ourselves privates in foot regiments. We search how we may see formal goodness in a life singularly inimical, hateful, to us.' Richard Aldington expresses the same dilemma in 'Living Sepulchres':

> One frosty night when the guns were still
> I leaned against the trench
> Making for myself hokku
> Of the moon and flowers and of the snow.
>
> But the ghostly scurrying of huge rats
> Swollen with feeding upon men's flesh
> Filled me with shrinking dread.

(Hokku is haiku – a short, very concentrated Japanese verse form, adopted by the Imagist poets.)

By 1916, the year of the Somme, Robert Graves (1895–1985, another of the Georgian poets and the author of *Goodbye To All That*) was already protesting strongly against the continuing public demand for gung-ho patriotic war poetry. In 'A Dead Boche' he speaks directly to those who only want to hear 'of blood and fame':

> I'll say (you've heard it said before)
>   'War's hell!' and if you doubt the same,
> To-day I found in Mametz Wood
> A certain cure for lust of blood:

The brusquely ironic tone ('A certain cure for lust of blood') of these lines does not prepare the reader for what follows. In a second stanza that confronts the horror of war head-on, Graves describes a German corpse:

Where, propped against a shattered trunk,
   In a great mess of things unclean,
Sat a dead Boche; he scowled and stunk
   With clothes and face a sodden green,
Big-bellied, spectacled, crop-haired,
Dribbling black blood from nose and beard.

The careful formal construction of this stanza allows no escape from the steady scrutiny of the dead man. Surrounded by an undefined 'great mess of things unclean' he still 'sat' and 'scowled'; but Graves's alliteration attaches to these actions of a living person the attributes of a corpse ('stunk ... sodden green'). No simile or metaphor is needed here to enhance the image. The corpse is still identifiable as a recently living individual by his spectacles and his hair-cut, but the 'black blood' of the final line turns him into an emblem of death in battle. There is no sign of mutual recognition or respect from one soldier to another (Graves does not hint at any such statement as 'I am the enemy you killed my friend' – the much-quoted line from Wilfred Owen's poem 'Strange Meeting') but the reader is challenged to disagree with Graves's claim that this is indeed a 'certain cure for lust of blood' – regardless of whose side you are on.

This stark delineation of the reality of war still has the power to appal today; in 1916 it did much to emphasise the growing distance between those at home who preferred to 'only hear of blood and fame' and those at the Front for whom such sights were becoming commonplace. This alienation affected writers as much as other members of the public. The Bloomsbury novelist and critic Virginia Woolf, a friend of Rupert Brooke and later of Siegfried Sassoon, felt:

> ... a mixture of a pacifist's horror of the glorification of militarism, and alienation from the ordinary combatant or civilian's view. The behaviour of most of her friends in wartime occupied this uneasy space between snobbish detachment and courageous resistance. Though they were naively unprepared for August 1914, when the war came they were in the vanguard of the peace movement, before a wider disillusionment with the war set in in 1916.
>
> (Hermione Lee *Virginia Woolf*, 1997)

This idea of 1916 as a watershed in the war was shared by many people, at least in retrospect; in many ways it marks a watershed in the poetry of the period, too. After the Battle of the Somme, which began on 1 July 1916 and finally dragged to a stalemate in November, the tenor of much of the poetry changed. The poems for which Wilfred Owen, Siegfried Sassoon and Edmund Blunden are best remembered, for instance, date from after this period. The poet David Jones explained the causes of this change in the Preface to *In Parenthesis*:

> This writing has to do with some things I saw, felt, & was part of. The period covered begins early in December 1915 and ends early in July 1916. The first date corresponds to my going to France. The latter roughly marks a change in the character of our lives in the infantry on the West Front. From then onwards things hardened into a more relentless, mechanical affair, took on a more sinister aspect. The wholesale slaughter of the later years, the conscripted levies filling the gaps in every file of four, knocked the bottom out of the intimate, continuing, domestic life of small contingents of men ... In the earlier months there was a certain attractive amateurishness, and elbow-room for idiosyncrasy that connected one with a less exacting past. ... How impersonal did each new draft seem arriving each month, and all these new-fangled gadgets to master.

▶ Choose and compare a selection of poems, some written before and some after 1916. Can you find in the post- July 1916 poems evidence to support David Jones's belief that life for the soldier became more 'relentless ... mechanical ... sinister ... impersonal'?

David Jones numbered himself among the 'amateur soldiers ... not only amateur, but grotesquely incompetent, a knocker-over of piles, a parade's despair' and Edmund Blunden called himself 'a harmless shepherd in a soldier's coat'. Richard Aldington, undergoing training in early 1916, wrote in 'Field Manoeuvres':

> I am 'to fire at the enemy column
> After it has passed' –
> But my obsolete rifle, loaded with 'blank',
> Lies untouched before me,
> My spirit follows after the gliding clouds ...

Such a note of self-conscious amateurism was no longer heard after the opening day of the Somme: 60,000 British troops were killed or wounded on 1 July 1916.

Women writers and the war 1914–16

During most of the 20th century, the assumption was that the essential literature of the First World War was written by men, that women's writing was inevitably less significant as an expression of the experience of war since only men had actually fought. Only one prose work by a woman, *Testament of Youth* by Vera Brittain, had established itself as part of the canon (see opposite) of Great War literature, and that was an autobiography, though it contained some of the author's poems, originally published under the title *Verses of a V.A.D.*. (Voluntary Aid Detachment – V.A.D.s were volunteer nurses).

Canon as a literary term means those texts and authors that are generally assumed to represent the writing of a particular period or **genre** or, indeed, of literature as a whole. Thus, to describe *Testament of Youth* as part of the canon is to suggest it is recognised as a book central to a discussion of Great War literature. The danger of literary canons is that they can seem to imply that texts which have not found a place (or have lost their place) on the canonical list are somehow less good, less important, less worth reading. This need not be so at all, and critics today often challenge the assumptions of the canon. (See also Part 2, pages 70–71.)

In fact, a great deal of the verse published during 1914–18 was written by women and much of it, when read today, adds a significant dimension to any discussion of the writing of the period. Most anthologies of war poetry have very few poems by women, but the publication in 1981 of Catherine Reilly's *Scars Upon My Heart*, an anthology subtitled *Women's Poetry and Verse of the First World War*, dramatically challenged the narrow assumption that war poetry could only reflect men's experience. The difficulty for women of being cut off from the 'men who march away' is reflected in this stanza from Nora Bomford's 'Drafts', a poem retrieved by Catherine Reilly from sixty years of obscurity and republished in *Scars Upon My Heart*:

> Waking to darkness; early silence broken
> By seagulls' cries, and something undefined
> And far away. Through senses half-awoken,
> A vague enquiry drifts into one's mind.
> What's happening? Down the hill a movement quickens
> And leaps to recognition round the turning –
> Then one's heart wakes, and grasps the fact, and sickens –
> 'Are we down-hearted' … 'Keep the homefires burning'.
> They go to God-knows-where, with songs of Blighty,
> While I'm in bed, and ribbons in my nightie.

The bathos of the final line and the absurd rhyme Blighty/nightie emphasises the speaker's sense of the frustration and even the indignity of not being able to share what men are going through.

As well as poems dealing with the war from the perspective of women, novels also appeared, though (like the prose works of authors such as Aldington, Blunden and Sassoon) these were often published ten years or more after the war had ended. These novels (for instance, Irene Rathbone's *We That Were Young*, 1932) usually began with the optimism of the pre-war period or the expectation that the war would be a short and decisive interlude in a period which was seeing positive changes for women.

In the years immediately before the war, the Suffragettes (campaigning for votes for women) had been part of a more general movement seeking a greater freedom for women than society generally allowed. Better access to education (especially to university education), more opportunities for women to undertake professional work, to participate in politics and to enjoy greater social independence – these were all issues that led people to take sides over the question of feminism: thus, Vera Brittain, her brother and her fiancé all called themselves feminists; by contrast, Rupert Brooke disliked the approval of feminism shown by nearly all his friends, men and women.

Women were heavily exploited as part of the recruitment and propaganda drives at the start of the war: the German invasion of neutral Belgium was presented as the 'rape' of a small, defenceless country and stories of the literal rape of Belgian women were quickly spread. In Britain, recruiting posters showed women pointing doubtful young men in the direction of France under the slogan 'Women of England Say Go' and a popular music-hall song had the raucous refrain:

> But on Saturday I'm willing,
> If you'll only take the shilling,
> To make a man of any one of you.

('Taking the king's shilling' meant 'joining the army'.)

More conventional wartime songs played heavily on the duty of women to support the morale of the men who were going to fight:

> Keep the home fires burning
> While we still are yearning ...

By no means all women or women writers shared these sentiments, however, and the feminist movement attracted a strong vein of pacifism: 'BETTER IS WISDOM THAN WEAPONS OF WAR' proclaimed a banner of the women students at Cambridge University, and the novelist Virginia Woolf shared the pacifist views of many of the Bloomsbury Group of writers and artists. Describing the impact of the war on women, Virginia Woolf wrote (in *A Room of One's Own*, 1929):

> Shall we lay the blame on the war? When the guns fired in 1914, did the faces of men and women show so plain in each other's eyes that romance was killed? Certainly it was a shock (to women in particular with their illusions about education, and so on) to see the faces of

our rulers in the light of the shell-fire. So ugly they looked – German, English, French – so stupid.

For many women writing about the war, however, the main themes were patience, loss and grief, and the experiences of the Front (the major subject of what most people still assume to be 'real' Great War poetry) could only be imagined.

▶ Look at the extract from *The Return of the Soldier* by Rebecca West and the poems by Marian Allen (Part 3, page 95 and page 75). How effectively is Rebecca West able to imagine the reality of trench life and No Man's Land? How do Marian Allen's sonnets convey the senses of loneliness and exclusion? Compare her poem 'Charing Cross' with Wilfred Owen's 'Spring Offensive'.

It is important to stress, though, that for many women, the war offered an opportunity to break out of the confines of their pre-1914 lives, often by taking on work that had previously been done by men and so earning higher wages than they had been able to do before. D.H. Lawrence's short story 'Tickets, Please' (1919) describes the girls who took over the jobs of the ticket collectors on the Nottingham trams during the war:

> This, the most dangerous tram-service in England, as the authorities themselves declare, with pride, is entirely conducted by girls, and driven by rash young men, a little crippled, or by delicate young men, who creep forward in terror. The girls are fearless young hussies. In their ugly blue uniform, skirts up to their knees, shapeless old peaked caps on their heads, they have all the *sang-froid* of an old non-commissioned officer. With a tram packed with howling colliers, roaring hymns downstairs and a sort of antiphony of obscenities upstairs, the lasses are perfectly at their ease. They pounce on the youths who try to evade their ticket machine. They push men off at the end of their distance. They are not going to be done in the eye – not they. They fear nobody – and everybody fears them.

The sense of social dislocation is neatly satirised in 'Sing a Song of War-Time' by Nina Macdonald, first published in *Wartime Nursery Rhymes* (1918) and rediscovered in *Scars Upon My Heart:*

> Mummie does the house-work,
> Can't get any maid,
> Gone to make munitions,
> 'Cause they're better paid,
> Nurse is always busy,

Never time to play,
Sewing shirts for soldiers,
Nearly ev'ry day.

Ev'ry body's doing
Something for the War,
Girls are doing things
They've never done before,
Go as 'bus conductors,
Drive a car or van,
All the world is topsy-turvy
Since the War began.

1916–18: the Somme and after

The Battle of the Somme has come to be seen as a watershed in the war – not so
much in a military sense (the battle went on until it ground to a halt in the mud in
mid-November) but because after 1916 the mood had changed and few shreds of
idealism remained. Conditions at home – rationing, air-raids – began to affect
morale as badly as the enormously long casualty lists printed each day in the
newspapers; at the Front, whether in France, Egypt, Mesopotamia or at sea, there
was a growing awareness of a gulf between those who did and those who did not
fight.

Much of the bitterness associated with the writing of the mainstream war poets
(e.g. Sassoon, Graves and Owen) belongs to this latter period of the war. But a
poem such as 'A Dead Boche' (see pages 24–25) is a reminder that, for the soldiers,
the disenchantment with patriotic militarism had already set in before the Somme.
Alongside this bitterness, though, was a strong sense that the war had to be
completed somehow. Very few of the writers at the Front, even those who came
close to pacifism, actually thought that they should themselves stop fighting once
they had become part of the army in the trenches. They thought the war was
appalling and were disgusted by the apparent lack of will to bring it to a halt:
Siegfried Sassoon risked being charged with treason by publishing a protest against
its continuation:

I am making this statement as an act of wilful defiance of military
authority, because I believe that the war is being deliberately
prolonged by those who have the power to end it.
I am a soldier, convinced that I am acting on behalf of soldiers.
I believe that this war, upon which I entered as a war of defence and
liberation, has now become a war of aggression and conquest.
I believe that the purposes for which I and my fellow-soldiers entered

upon this war should have been so clearly stated as to have made it impossible to change them, and that, had this been done, the objects which actuated us would now be attainable by negotiation.

I have seen and endured the sufferings of the troops, and I can no longer be a party to prolong these sufferings for ends which I believe to be evil and unjust.

I am not protesting against the conduct of the war, but against the political errors and insincerities for which the fighting men are being sacrificed.

On behalf of those who are suffering now I make this protest against the deception which is being practised on them; also I believe that I may help to destroy the callous complacence with which the majority of those at home regard the continuance of agonies which they do not share, and which they have not sufficient imagination to realize.

This protest, which led to Sassoon's being treated for 'shell-shock' at Craiglockhart Hospital, Edinburgh, where he met Wilfred Owen, was published in July 1917. (Two accounts of the story and its consequences are important Great War texts: the first is the autobiographical *Goodbye to All That* (1929) by Robert Graves; the second is the novel *Regeneration* (1991) by Pat Barker.)

Isaac Rosenberg (unlike Sassoon, a private soldier) found himself almost dehumanised by the experience of war, unable to do anything for himself. In a letter of February 1918 he wrote 'Sometimes I give way and am appalled at the devastation this life seems to have made in my nature. It seems to have blunted me.' In another letter of the same month, he wrote:

All the poetry has gone quite out of me. I seem even to forget words, and I believe if I met anybody with ideas I'd be dumb. No drug could be more stupefying than our work (to me anyway), and this goes on like that old torture of water trickling, drop by drop unendingly, on one's helplessness.

When Wilfred Owen returned to France in August 1918, having written nearly all of the poems for which he is now remembered, he wrote to Sassoon: 'Everything is clear now; & I'm in hasty retreat towards the Front. Battle is easier here; and therefore you will stay and endure old men and women to the End [Sassoon had been wounded and was in hospital in London], and wage the bitterer war and more hopeless.'

▶ Here is the Preface drafted by Wilfred Owen for the volume of his poems that he had prepared but did not live to see published. What do you gather from it about Owen's view of poetry and the Great War, and of his attitude to the war itself?

> This book is not about heroes. English poetry is not yet fit to speak of them.
>
> Nor is it about deeds, or lands, nor anything about glory, honour, might, majesty, dominion, or power, except War.
>
> Above all I am not concerned with Poetry.
>
> My subject is War, and the pity of War.
>
> The Poetry is in the pity.
>
> Yet these elegies are to this generation in no sense consolatory. They may be to the next. All a poet can do today is warn. That is why the true Poets must be truthful.
>
> If I thought the letter of this book would last, I might have used proper names; but if the spirit of it survives – survives Prussia – my ambition and those names will have achieved themselves fresher fields than Flanders.

▶ Some critics and editors refer to the 'trench poets', to distinguish those who actually wrote about the fighting from their first-hand experience. How important do you think it is to make this distinction in a discussion of the poetry of the Great War today?

Wilfred Owen was killed in battle on 4 November 1918, a week before the Armistice. It is interesting to speculate what would have become of his reputation had he survived and not become – for the public and for his own fellow-poets (see Part 3, pages 74 and 77) – the representative voice of all who had died between 1914–18. For those poets who were still at the Front on 11 November 1918, the end of the fighting at first brought simply relief:

> One got peace of heart at last, the dark march over,
> And the straps slipped, the warmth felt under roof's low cover,
> Lying slack the body, let sink in straw giving;
> And some sweetness, a great sweetness felt in mere living ...
>
> (Ivor Gurney 'After War')

Almost at once, however, the emotions became more complex: Siegfried Sassoon dealt with the difficult problem of attitudes to Germany, in 'Reconciliation', a poem written in the month of the Armistice and addressed to the mothers of English soldiers now able to go and visit the graves of their sons:

When you are standing at your hero's grave,
Or near some homeless village where he died,
Remember, through your heart's rekindling pride,
The German soldiers who were loyal and brave.
Men fought like brutes; and hideous things were done;
And you have nourished hatred, harsh and blind.
But in that Golgotha perhaps you'll find
The mothers of the men who killed your son.

It is hard to imagine, today, how people in 1918 would have reacted to a line such as 'you have nourished hatred, harsh and blind', but only Sassoon's refusal to be tactful at this moment makes it possible for readers (then and now) to see the full force of the poem's title 'Reconciliation'. The last two lines of this poem stand alongside the famous closing statement from Wilfred Owen's 'Strange Meeting':

I am the enemy you killed, my friend.
Let us sleep now ...

Adjustment to a post-war world was going to be difficult for men and women alike; uncertainty about the future is demonstrated in both poetry and prose:

... I am too restless
For the old life,
Too contemptuous of narrow shoulders
To sit again with the café-chatterers,
Too sick at heart with overmuch slaughter
To dream quietly over books ...

                              (Richard Aldington 'Meditation')

In the novel *Death of a Hero* (1929), Aldington resolved this dilemma for the main character, George Winterbourne, by having him deliberately get machine-gunned in the closing moments of the war. For women there was no such fictional let-out. Vera Brittain, in *Testament of Youth*, described her emotions on the evening of 11 November:

After the long, long blackness, it seemed like a fairy-tale to see the street lamps shining through the chill November gloom. I detached myself from the others and walked slowly up Whitehall, with my heart sinking in a sudden cold dismay. Already this was a different world from the one that I had known during four life-long years, a world in which people would be light-hearted and forgetful, in which themselves and their careers and amusements would blot out

political ideals and great national issues. And in that brightly lit, alien
world I should have no part.

The next section of her book, dealing with life immediately after the war, she
entitled 'Survivors Not Wanted'. It was a title many survivors of the war would have
echoed with increasing bitterness during the coming decade.

Writing in the aftermath of the Great War

War is another world, where men feel and act differently; and so,
when they return to the other world of peace and ordinariness, they
feel a need to tell their tales of the somewhere else where they have
been. In memory, war seems like a dream, or the life of some other
man, remembered with a kind of astonishment.

(Samuel Hynes *The Soldiers' Tale,* 1997)

The need to tell their tales, to make sense of the 'somewhere else where they have
been', was for many men and women a necessary part of the process of adjusting to
post-war life. It is often remarked that it took at least ten years for most of the post-
war memoirs and novels to appear, as if a decade of gestation had been necessary.
For some of the writers, the shaping of memory into fictional or semi-fictional form
(books such as Sassoon's *Memoirs of an Infantry Officer* span the genres of fiction
and autobiography) was the last stage in a process of recovery from what is today
recognised as post-traumatic stress: the obsessive need to revisit the memories of
horror and distress, recurrent nightmares, the sense of overwhelming guilt at
having survived an experience which others did not. Richard Aldington spoke in his
autobiography, *Life for Life's Sake*, of 'having purged his bosom of perilous stuff'
by writing *Death of a Hero*, and a short story he wrote a decade after the war was
called 'Farewell to Memories' as if he was at last able to shake off the guilt that had
clung to him like the albatross round the neck of the Ancient Mariner (see Part 3,
pages 73–74).

D.H. Lawrence drew on his friendship with Aldington for a passage in his novel
Aaron's Rod (1922) in which he describes two men, Herbertson and Lilly,
discussing the war:

And then Herbertson was on the subject he was obsessed by. He
had come, unconsciously, for this and this only; to talk war to Lilly:
or at Lilly ... it was a driving instinct – to come and get it off his chest ...
and every time it was the same thing, the same hot, blind, anguished
voice of a man who has seen too much, experienced too much, and
doesn't know where to turn. None of the glamour of returned heroes,

none of the romance of war: only a hot, blind, mesmerised voice, going on and on, mesmerised by a vision that the soul cannot bear.

When Herbertson eventually leaves, Lilly (based on Lawrence himself) complains that the war was 'all unreal ... not as real as a bad dream. Why the hell don't they wake up and realise it!' For Aldington, the waking up from the nightmare was only to be achieved through writing. In 'Eumenides', published in 1923 in a volume called *Exile*, he describes how the same memories of the trenches keep coming back to him night after night:

> O the thousand images I see
> And struggle with and cannot kill –
>
> It is all so stale,
> It has been said a thousand times;
> Millions have seen it, been it, as I;
> Millions may have been haunted by these spirits
> As I am haunted ...

He tries to define why he is being haunted in this way by the Eumenides (in the ancient Greek drama *Oresteia* by Aeschylus, the Eumenides are the Furies who pursue Orestes for killing his mother Clytemnestra); and reaches an unexpected conclusion:

> What is it I agonise for?
> The dead? They are quiet;
> They can have no complaint.
> No, it is my own murdered self –
> A self which had its passion for beauty,
> Some moment's touch with immortality –
> Violently slain, which rises up like a ghost
> To torment my nights,
> To pain me.
> It is myself that is the Eumenides,
> That will not be appeased, about my bed;
> It is the wrong that has been done me
> Which none has atoned for, none repented of,
> Which rises before me, demanding atonement.
>
> Tell me, what answer shall I give my murdered self?

This is clearly a very personal, even self-obsessed, response to surviving the war, but its emphasis on nightmare and on the fragmentation of experience ('the thousand images I see') become central to post-war writing. The American poet Ezra Pound demonstrated this in 'Hugh Selwyn Mauberley', a poem in which he sums up his feelings at the end of the war. For what had so many people died? he asks, and concludes:

> There died a myriad,
> And of the best among them,
> For an old bitch gone in the teeth,
> For a botched civilisation ...
>
> For two gross of broken statues,
> For a few thousand battered books.

This idea of fragmentation is also at the heart of the most influential of all poems reflecting on life in the aftermath of the war, T.S. Eliot's *The Waste Land* (1922). Eliot himself had, like his fellow American Ezra Pound, spent the war in London and his long poem moves backwards and forwards in time ('mixing memory and desire') in an attempt to understand how the modern world has created a waste land out of so rich a cultural and spiritual heritage:

> What are the roots that clutch, what branches grow
> Out of this stony rubbish? Son of man,
> You cannot say, or guess, for you know only
> A heap of broken images, where the sun beats,
> And the dead tree gives no shelter, the cricket no relief,
> And the dry stone no sound of water.

Eliot's original plan had been to call the poem 'He Do the Police in Different Voices' (a quotation from one of Dickens' most famous London novels, *Our Mutual Friend*) and much of *The Waste Land* is made up of conversations – themselves often fragmented, reflecting the nervous exhaustion and fear of the survivors of the war, both soldier and civilian. In the second section of the poem, 'A Game of Chess' a woman speaks to a man:

> 'My nerves are bad tonight. Yes, bad. Stay with me.
> Speak to me. Why do you never speak? Speak.
> What are you thinking of? What thinking? What?
> I never know what you are thinking. Think.'

The man's reply could suggest that his thoughts are still fixed in the trenches:

> I think we are in rats' alley
> Where the dead men lost their bones.

Later in 'A Game of Chess' the focus shifts to a dockside pub where a group of Eastend women are discussing a soldier's return from the war:

> and think of poor Albert,
> He's been in the army four years, he wants a good time,
> And if you don't give it him, there's others will, I said.
> Oh is there, she said. Something o' that, I said.

These brief illustrations of the snatches of conversation in the poem suggest how the whole structure of *The Waste Land* is fragmented, reflecting its themes and post-war perspectives. It is as if the poem is an accumulation of voices and images half remembered from a bad dream. This way of writing is quite different from that of the Georgian poets before and during 1914–18; it indicates how a modernist poem offered opportunities for exploring the social, cultural and moral disintegration caused by war which traditional forms and voices could not match.

The different voices of *The Waste Land* are a reminder that in prose, too, the authentic voice of the individual recalling his or her own wartime and post-war experiences is rarely presented as strict autobiography. Richard Aldington wrote extensively about the war in poetry, short stories and novels, but when he later wrote his memoirs he deliberately omitted any account of his life as a soldier on the grounds that he had already said everything he had to say on the subject. Robert Graves presented *Goodbye to All That* (1929) as autobiography (and indeed the book traces his life from his schooldays through to the later 1920s) but he was careful to distinguish between what was 'true' and what was 'truthful':

> It was practically impossible (as well as forbidden) to keep a diary in any active trench-sector, or to send letters home which would be of any great post-War documentary value; and the more efficient the soldier the less time, of course, he took from his job to write about it. Great latitude should therefore be allowed to a soldier who has since got his facts or dates mixed. I would even paradoxically say that the memoirs of a man who went through some of the worst experiences of trench warfare are not truthful if they do not contain a high proportion of falsities.
>
> (quoted in Samuel Hynes *The Soldiers' Tale*)

No writer spent longer reflecting on, and reconstructing, his wartime experience than Siegfried Sassoon. He continued to write poetry about the difficulty of shaping his memories of war:

Remembering, we forget
Much that was monstrous, much that clogged our souls with clay ...

(This poem, 'To One Who Was With Me in the War', is printed in full on page 92.)
He wrote a fictionalised autobiography of his war, *Memoirs of an Infantry Officer*
(1930), in which he presents himself as a rather naive young countryman, George
Sherston; then, during the Second World War, he returned to the subject yet again
and in 1945 published a 'straight' autobiography, *Siegfried's Journey, 1916–1920*.
But Sassoon was aware that even this book belonged to the category of writing
Graves had described as 'truthful, not true'. In the final pages he wrote:

> It needs no pointing out that there is an essential disparity between
> being alive and memorizing about it long afterwards. But the
> recorder of his vanished self must also bear this in mind, that his
> passage through time was a confused experiment, and that external
> circumstances had yet to become static and solidly discernible ... In
> relation to his surroundings my younger self seemed to be watching a
> play performed in a language of which he couldn't understand more
> than an occasional word. His apprehensions of the contemporary
> scene were blinkered, out of focus, and amorphous as the imagery of
> a dream. I have felt that throughout the journey described in this
> book he was like someone driving a motor-car on a foggy night, only
> able to see a few yards in front of him. Nevertheless I have contrived
> to reconstruct an outline which represents everything as though it
> had been arranged for him beforehand.

▶ Look at the ways in which Sassoon describes the problems of writing about his
past wartime self in this passage. Are these descriptions (a play in a strange
language, 'blinkered, out of focus ... the imagery of a dream', a journey on a foggy
night) helpful in trying to understand how other writers made sense of their
wartime experience?

Another writer who understood the problem of keeping memories of the war in
focus was Edmund Blunden. In a poem 'Can You Remember?' (published in 1937)
he wrote:

> Yes, I still remember
>   The whole thing in a way;
> Edge and exactitude
>   Depend on the day.

The speaker admits that some details of his memory are fading –

> ... commonly I fail to name
>   That once obvious Hill,
> And where we went and whence we came
>   To be killed, or kill ...

– but they can easily be retrieved:

> ... at the instance
>   Of sound, smell, change and stir,
> New-old shapes for ever
>   Intensely recur.

The intensity with which these 'new-old shapes' came back to haunt Blunden made it impossible to put the memory of war aside, and in any case much of the work he was to do in the 1920s and beyond kept it vividly alive for him: in addition to writing his own memoirs, *Undertones of War* (1928) he also edited the poetry of Wilfred Owen and, later, of Ivor Gurney. With the approach of the Second World War he felt an increasing need to ensure that what the war poets had said should not be ignored by the next generation. Owen's remark in his Preface (see page 32) 'All a poet can do today is warn' haunted Blunden as much as the memory of war itself, and in his poem 'To W.O. and his Kind' (i.e. the other poets who had died in the Great War) Blunden asked:

> What hope is there? What harvest from those hours
> Deliberately, and in the name of truth,
> Endured by you? Your witness moves no Powers,
> And younger youth resents your sentient youth.

▶ Read Blunden's poems 'To W.O. and His Kind' and 'To Wilfred Owen' (Part 3, page 77). How would you sum up Owen's importance for Blunden and the importance, as Blunden saw it, of Owen to others? Contrast the ways Blunden and Aldington wrote about Owen by comparing these poems with Aldington's 'In Memory of Wilfred Owen' (page 74).

Aside from the writing of those who had actually been at the Front, the Great War featured prominently in the fiction and (importantly but less prominently) in the drama of the 1920s and 1930s. Its devastating effect on a whole generation is summed up in the fiction of Virginia Woolf. Her novel *Jacob's Room* (begun in 1920, published 1922) presents the optimism of pre-war youth destroyed by notions of honour and Englishness that Woolf herself viewed with anger and despair:

The battleships ray out over the North Sea, keeping their stations
accurately apart. At a given signal all the guns are trained on a target
which (the master gunner counts in seconds, watch in hand – at the
sixth he looks up) flames into splinters. With equal nonchalance a
dozen young men in the prime of life descend with composed faces
into the depths of the sea; and there impassively (though with
perfect mastery of machinery) suffocate uncomplainingly together.
Like blocks of tin soldiers the army covers the cornfield, moves up
the hillside, stops, reels slightly this way and that, and falls flat, save
that, through field-glasses, it can be seen that one or two pieces still
agitate up and down like fragments of broken match-stick.

Woolf's anger is directed at the dehumanisation caused by war and by the attitudes
that train young men to die 'uncomplainingly'. Her contempt for the political
processes that have led to the war is witheringly expressed in her next sentence:
'These actions, together with the incessant commerce of banks, laboratories,
chancellories, and houses of business, are the strokes which oar the world forward,
they say.' Meanwhile, the war – in which the young Jacob is going to die before he
can achieve any of the things he is destined for – intrudes even on rural domestic
life in England. Virginia Woolf's writing juxtaposes the distant menace of the guns
with the ordinary details of everyday living:

'The guns?' said Betty Flanders, half asleep, getting out of bed and
going to the window, which was decorated with a fringe of dark
leaves.
'Not at this distance,' she thought. 'It is the sea.'
Again, far away, she heard the dull sound, as if nocturnal women
were beating great carpets. There was Morty lost, and Seabrook
dead; her sons fighting for their country. But were the chickens safe?
Was that someone moving downstairs? Rebecca with the toothache?
No. The nocturnal women were beating great carpets. Her hens
shifted slightly on their perches.

The Great War on stage

Probably the most enduringly popular play to be written about the war has been
Journey's End (1928) by R.C. Sherriff, who had fought in France. Set in a dug-out
in the trenches, it explores the tensions between a group of officers waiting for an
attack. The names of the characters (Stanhope, Osborne, Raleigh, etc.) emphasise
their essential Englishness, and their public school background provides the
context for the social tensions that provide as much of the drama as the war itself.
    Three other plays, however, also make a significant contribution to the writing

of this period. The first two were written during the war but not published until afterwards. John Drinkwater, a member of the Dymock poets (see page 18 and Glossary) and a leading figure in the revival of English verse drama, wrote a one-act play called x = o, whose strongly pacifist message was disguised behind its setting: the Trojan War. The play offers a parallel between two wars which began with a clear enough purpose but which had become meaningless to those who had to fight:

> SALVIUS   How should we hate the dead?
> And, where death ranges as among us now,
> You, Pronax, I, and our antagonists
> And friends alike are all but as dead men
> Moving together in a ghostly world,
> With life a luckless beggar at the door.

In a series of short scenes, young soldiers from both sides discuss the pointlessness of the war and its disruptive effect on their lives as aspiring writers, artists and politicians (see Part 3, page 79). Committed to continuing to fight for their countries, one of the Greek soldiers kills a Trojan and one of the Trojans kills a Greek in night sorties – their deaths cancelling each other out, hence the title of the play. With its classical setting and blank verse, the play today seems a curiously oblique commentary on the war, but it was first performed in 1917 at a time when its arguments (not dissimilar to the propositions in Siegfried Sassoon's 'A Soldier's Statement' for which he was expecting to be court-martialled) could probably not have been presented more directly on the English stage.

For the same reasons, George Bernard Shaw withheld his play *Heartbreak House* until the end of the war. It was first performed in 1919 and its publication was (as always with Shaw) an opportunity for the playwright to discuss its themes in a polemical Preface. The Preface to *Heartbreak House* is one of the most scathing attacks on the hypocrisy of English attitudes to the war ever published:

> When nearly every house had a slaughtered son to mourn, we should all have gone quite out of our senses if we had taken our own and our friends' bereavements at their peace value. It became necessary to give them a false value; to proclaim the young life worthily and gloriously sacrificed to redeem the liberty of mankind, instead of to expiate the heedlessness and folly of their fathers, and expiate it in vain. We had even to assume that the parents and not the children had made the sacrifice, until at last the comic papers were driven to satirise fat old men, sitting comfortably in club chairs, and boasting of the sons they had 'given' to their country …

This hypocrisy Shaw identified as coming from England's pre-war complacency, and it is that sense of self-righteousness and self-satisfaction which *Heartbreak House* itself exposes. The play ends with the house ('this ship we are all in ... this soul's prison we call England') being bombed in an air-raid, and with Ellie, the play's idealistic young heroine, hoping that the Zeppelin will return again the following night to destroy the house completely.

▶ In the Preface to *Heartbreak House*, Shaw wrote: 'To the truly civilised man, to the good European, the slaughter of German youth was as disastrous as the slaughter of the English. Fools exulted in "German losses". They were our losses as well. Imagine exulting in the death of Beethoven because Bill Sykes [the villainous thug in Dickens' novel *Oliver Twist*] dealt him his death blow!' How far does the idea of 'the good European' feature in the writing about the Great War you have encountered? In the light of Shaw's remarks, read the extract from Drinkwater's *x=o* on page 79. How much common ground do you find between the two playwrights?

The third play that focuses specifically on the Great War and its effects on post-war England is *For Services Rendered* (1932) by Somerset Maugham (see Part 3, pages 85–86). The title ironically asks what rewards and honours have really been bestowed on those who fought. For each of the main characters life after the war has been at best a disappointment and at worst a cheat. This disillusionment destroys the Ardsley family, middle class and outwardly content, when their son Sydney, blinded in the trenches ten years earlier, speaks out:

> You see, I feel I have a certain right to speak. I know how dead keen we all were when the war started. Every sacrifice was worth it. We didn't say much about it because we were rather shy, but honour did mean something to us and patriotism wasn't just a word.

Having described the initial naive enthusiasm he and his contemporaries had felt, Sydney turns to attack the politicians – not just of England but of Europe – for allowing the war to happen in the first place:

> I know we were the dupes of the incompetent fools who ruled the nations. I know that we were sacrificed to their vanity, their greed and their stupidity. And the worst of it is that as far as I can tell they haven't learnt a thing.

This last point introduces an important feature of the way the Great War was used in the writing of the 1920s and particularly of the 1930s: as the political situation in

Europe began to deteriorate, writers started to use the Great War as a reminder of the lessons from the past they feared had not been learned. In *For Services Rendered* both Sydney's father and Howard, an ex-soldier who 'had the time of my life in the war', look forward to the possibility that there might be another chance to do their duty or to get back into uniform To his elderly father's fatuous statement 'And if I'm wanted again I shall be ready again', Sydney can only mutter between his teeth 'God give me patience'.

▶ Compare the extract from *For Services Rendered* (pages 85–86) with the following passage from Aldington's *Death of a Hero* (1929). How closely do you think Maugham and Aldington agree about the war, and how effectively does each present his argument?

> When I meet an unmaimed man of my generation, I want to shout at him: 'How did you escape? How did you dodge it? What dirty trick did you play? Why are you not dead, trickster?' It is dreadful to have outlived your life, to have shirked your fate, to have overspent your welcome ... You, the war dead, I think you died in vain, I think you died for nothing, for a blast of wind, a blather, a humbug, a newspaper stunt, a politician's ramp. But at least you died ... You chose the better part.

It is significant that the approach of the Second World War brought a renewed sense of defeat to those writers who had survived the First and had tried through their writing to do what Wilfred Owen had said poets should do, 'to warn'. Edmund Blunden was accused of having pro-German sympathies, because he spoke out against rearmament; Richard Aldington left Europe altogether; Siegfried Sassoon spent 1939–45 revisiting the Great War by writing his autobiography of 1916–20. Herbert Read spoke perhaps for all of them in his poem 'To a Conscript of 1940' (see Part 3, page 88):

> I am one of those who went before you
> Five-and-twenty years ago: one of the many who never returned,
> Of the many who returned and yet were dead.
>
> We went where you are going, into the rain and the mud;
> We fought as you will fight
> With death and darkness and despair;
> We gave what you will give – our brains and our blood.
>
> We think we gave in vain. The world was not renewed ...

Reviving the memory of the Great War

It is not surprising that in the aftermath of the Second World War there should have been less focus on the First. During 1939–45 there had been a sense of shocked awareness that a war needed poets and 'Where are the war poets?' became a stock question. In fact, there were poets and novelists who saw themselves following in the tradition of the writers of the Great War: Keith Douglas, for instance, wrote in one of his poems, 'Rosenberg, I only repeat what you were saying'. But during the 1950s and 1960s the literary and cultural preoccupations were more to do with the post-war world. Writers who had survived the Great War and were still publishing new work had long since ceased to be at the centre of any literary movement: Graves, living in Majorca, continued to publish poetry that was widely admired but had little influence on younger writers; Blunden had published an edition of the poetry of Ivor Gurney in 1954 but it had attracted little attention, and his own pastoral style seemed to belong to an altogether different world; and when Aldington published a biography of T.E. Lawrence (*Lawrence of Arabia: A Biographical Enquiry*, 1955), demonstrating that many of the stories attached to this hero of the Great War were lies and myth-making, he was savagely denounced.

Two linked factors, however, brought about a revival of interest in the Great War and in writing about it. First, by the 1960s the events of 1914–18 had become sufficiently historical to feature in school and university history syllabuses. Hence new books began to be written about the war and a new interest in the whole period led to a revival of the literature associated with it. At the same time, the peace movements in Britain and throughout Europe and America were starting to attract significant numbers of people (especially young people), first in protest against nuclear weapons (for example CND – the Campaign for Nuclear Disarmament) and then against United States' involvement in Vietnam. This led to a renewed interest in the poetry of Owen, Sassoon and the other poets whose work was now seen a protest against war itself, not just against the conditions of the First World War.

In 1962, the English composer Benjamin Britten was commissioned to write a new work for the opening celebrations of the new Coventry Cathedral. The old cathedral had been bombed in 1940, and since 1945 its ruins had become a powerful symbol of reconciliation. Britten's *War Requiem* was an immediately influential restatement of the idea of war's waste and devastation. Britten was himself a pacifist and chose to combine the traditional Latin mass for the dead (the Requiem) with text from the poetry of Wilfred Owen, beginning with 'My subject is War and the Pity of War'.

The persistence of the Great War in the memory and in the imagination can be seen in the poems written in the 1950s and 1960s by English writers who could remember the Second World War but not the First. Vernon Scannell, who had been born in 1922 and served in North Africa and France between 1940–45, expressed this in 'The Great War':

> Whenever war is spoken of
> I find
> The War that was called Great invades the mind ...

The images that come to him are not images from his own experience of war, but from a war that had fascinated him from childhood onwards:

> And now,
> Whenever the November sky
> Quivers with a bugle's hoarse, sweet cry,
> The reason darkens; in its evening gleam
> Crosses and flares, tormented wire, grey earth
> Splattered with crimson flowers,
> And I remember,
> Not the war I fought in
> But the one called Great
> Which ended in a sepia November
> Four years before my birth.

▶ Compare these lines with other poems written about Remembrance Day and war memorials (for instance 'The Cenotaph' by Charlotte Mew, and 'On Passing the New Menin Gate' by Siegfried Sassoon (Part 3, page 86, page 92). How important is the different time perspective in each of these poems? How does it influence the way a reader today might respond to them?

Scannell's phrase, 'a sepia November' is a reminder that so many of the images of the soldiers from the Great War, as well as images of the trenches and No Man's Land, have survived in faded photographs. The very act of fading into a brown tinge of sepia endows such images with a sense of the past remembered, even with a degree of nostalgia for a vanished world. A powerful poem by Ted Hughes (1930–98), 'Six Young Men' explores precisely this point:

> The celluloid of a photograph holds them well –
> Six young men, familiar to their friends.

Hughes insists that the photograph must not be allowed to disguise the reality of what happened to these six young men, all of whom were killed:

Here, see a man's photograph,
The locket of a smile, turned overnight
Into the hospital of his mangled last
Agony and hours; see bundled in it
His mightier-than-man dead bulk and weight:
And on this one place which keeps him alive
(In his Sunday best) see fall war's worst
Thinkable flash and rending, onto his smile
Forty years rotting in the soil.

By forcing the reader to confront the reality behind the image ('Here, see') Hughes is able to juxtapose 'the locket [itself an image of memory] of a smile' with 'his mangled last Agony', and 'his Sunday best' [clothes] with his 'smile Forty years rotting in the soil'. The reader whom Hughes addresses is, like himself, a member of a younger generation, someone whose images of the Great War are all second-hand. His poem is about remembrance, and about the need to remember with accuracy, not with nostalgia.

Nostalgia and the Great War

Yet, in a sense the nostalgia is also part of the memory of the Great War. From August 1914 onwards, every grieving family experienced both loss and regret; and this regret, a realisation that you cannot retrieve what it is you have lost, is a powerful element of nostalgia. It provokes a yearning for the past as it was. In the years following the Armistice there was a growing awareness that 'the world would never be the same again', that 1914–18 cut the modern world off from the world as it had been before. It was easy to see the past as a golden age, whose innocence had been destroyed by the horrors of the trenches. Such a view was undoubtedly an oversimplification, if it had been true at all, but it too has become part of the way the Great War is remembered, as Philip Larkin's poem 'MCMXIV' (published in *The Whitsun Weddings*, 1967) demonstrates:

Never such innocence,
Never before or since,
As changed itself to past
Without a word – the men
Leaving the gardens tidy,
The thousands of marriages,
Lasting a little while longer:
Never such innocence again.

The Great War in British fiction 1960–95

The 20th century ended with a collection of new novels firmly located in the Great War. A number of key novels written earlier in the century were also reissued or published for the first time. In 1960 H.D.'s *Bid Me To Live*, a novel probably begun in 1918, then written and revised over the next forty years, presented a vivid and disturbing picture of life in London during 1914–18. H.D. (Hilda Doolittle) was an American poet who had come to London before the First World War, and had been one of the original Imagist poets (see page 16 and Glossary) and was an influential figure in the literary circle that centred on Ezra Pound. She married the poet Richard Aldington, and it is the collapse of their relationship under the strain of war which is at the heart of the book.

Aldington in the novel is presented as Rafe Allen, training to be a signals and intelligence officer, stationed at first in various parts of England (Sussex, Kent, the North) and only sent to France for the final year of fighting. As he becomes more and more immersed in the preparations that will take him to France, his relationship with the writers and artists who have been his friends and companions deteriorates and they find him 'less interesting' than before. His wife finds the strain of his being in the army in England, but always on the point of being posted abroad, intolerable: 'Guns! guns! guns!' she cries as yet another weapons course delays his departure. After Christmas 1917, he is expecting finally to be sent to France and there is another delay. Echoing her earlier cry, his wife screams 'Go! go! go! go!' even though they both realise the chances of his surviving are slight.

Three things make *Bid Me to Live* important in the context of the Great War in British literature. First, it was written about the First World War through the filter of the Second (H.D. had spent the whole of 1939–45 in England and had lived through the Blitz in London). It becomes, therefore, a study of the impact of war in general as much as of the Great War in particular, while still being located in the events of 1914–18. It has, secondly, become an important text for those concerned with a feminist critique of the Great War (see Part 4, pages 102–106), a penetrating study of men and women under the strain of war as seen from a woman's perspective. Third, it is an interesting and valuable exercise to compare H.D's account with Aldington's own, as presented in *Death of a Hero* (first published in 1929).

Death of a Hero was reissued in the 1960s and widely translated, as was Aldington's second novel, *The Colonel's Daughter* (1931) a satire on post-war England. Other novels about the Great War that had been a long time in gestation or were reissued (all contributing to the revival of interest in the literature of the period as well as the period in literature) included a sequence of novels by Henry Williamson (*A Chronicle of Ancient Sunlight*, 1951–69) and *We That Were Young* (first published 1932) by Irene Rathbone (see Part 3, pages 87–88, and Part 4, pages 104–106).

The most significant new novel, however, was *Strange Meeting* by Susan Hill, published in 1971. Taking its title from Wilfred Owen's poem, Hill's novel centres on the friendship of two young officers, Hilliard and Barton, whose very English names and backgrounds emphasise that the book is concerned with the idea of Englishness as defined in the behaviour of men under stress at the Front. At the time of its publication, to write a novel about intense relationships between men in the First World War was considered an ambitious risk for a woman writer. If nothing else, Hill proved that this was patronising prejudice and that the idea of the war as belonging somehow only to men could be challenged.

Like any other writer of her generation (she was born in 1942), she had to rely on her own research and reading to ensure that the setting and details of her scenes set in France were accurate. She has said that the initial impetus to write about the Great War came after hearing a performance of Benjamin Britten's *War Requiem* in 1962. For the next eight years she put off the idea because she was frightened by:

> ... the knowledge that I should have to sink myself completely and utterly in imagination, in emotions, into the experience of that awful war. In writing about it, I realised that a big piece of my own self would somehow disappear, I should never be quite the same again.
>
> (from the Introduction to *Strange Meeting*,
> Longman *Imprint* edition, 1984)

Her rationalisation of why she should nevertheless write the book throws an interesting light on why the Great War continues to fascinate and challenge writers and readers:

> But if we are to grow – and I am sure that is what we are meant to do, that is the point of our existence – we must change, we have to learn things, and also give things up, and those things include the cosiness of ignorance and the safety of detachment. To understand the present ... we have to know it, face it and accept it, and be hurt and personally changed, too, by various aspects of the truth.

It was for these reasons that Susan Hill decided to approach writing a novel about the Great War, and her experience in researching and then writing *Strange Meeting* was every bit as difficult as she had anticipated. It was:

> ... a terrible world to enter, imaginatively, an appalling business to be with young soldiers, day and night, in the trenches and in battle, in danger and fear and dirt. I felt exhausted, tense, horrified, depressed and angry the whole time. At the end I felt drained.

In *Birdsong* (1993) Sebastian Faulks explores the compulsion to research the Great War as well as the war itself. The novel moves between the historic past (it begins in France in 1910, then jumps to 1916 and the Battle of the Somme) and the contemporary world of 1978 in which an English woman, Elizabeth Benson, tries to make contact with survivors of the Great War. After discovering the diary of her grandfather who had fought in France and had died before she was born, Elizabeth goes in search of anyone still alive who might have known him. Her quest takes her eventually to an asylum where she finds one of the soldiers who had served with her grandfather. This man had been wounded and shell-shocked in October 1918 and had spent the rest of his life in this institution. His last visitor had come in 1949. He has no clear memories of the war, only of a street party after the Relief of Mafeking; he makes only a passing reference which may or may not be to Elizabeth's grandfather. What knowledge he still has of the war, if any, is securely locked inside him.

This sense of the survivors locking away their knowledge is an important theme in the book. Later Elizabeth discovers among her grandfather's papers ('finally she had what she wanted: the past was alive in the spidery letters in her slightly shaking hand') a diary entry which reads:

> Men come out from England like emissaries from an unknown land. I cannot picture what it means to be at peace. I do not know how people there can lead a life.
>
> The only things that sometimes jolt us back from this trance are memories of men. In the set of the eyes of some conscripted boy I see a look of Douglas or [name illeg. Reeve?] I find myself rigid with imagining. I can see that man's skull opening as he bent down to his friend that summer morning ...
>
> I do not know what I have done to live in this existence. I do not know what any of us did to tilt the world into this unnatural orbit. We came here only for a few months.
>
> No child or future generation will ever know what this was like. They will never understand.
>
> When it is over we will go quietly among the living and we will not tell them.

Elizabeth later learns that when her grandfather had come back from the war, he did not speak at all for two years.

Yet, *Birdsong* is not only about the silence of the survivors, for the larger part of the book deals with the experiences of Stephen Wraysford (Elizabeth's grandfather) in France. Faulks presents all the familiar landscapes – the trenches, No Man's land, behind the lines, the Field Hospital – with an astonishing intensity, and his set-piece account of the opening minutes of the Battle of the Somme stands as one of the most powerful accounts of the battle to be written.

Although Wraysford is an officer, he is not a typical English ex-public school lieutenant; indeed he had been living in France before the war with no home or family in England to return to. In this respect Faulks' book differs significantly from, say, *Strange Meeting*; and Wraysford's sympathy for the men under his command, miners from Yorkshire drafted in as sappers to dig mines under the enemy lines is powerfully demonstrated at the end of the novel when he is trapped with one of the miners underground and the miner, Jack Firebrace, is killed in an explosion that entombs both of them. He is eventually rescued by three German soldiers, one of them a Jew, Levi, whose brother has been killed in the same explosion. As they emerge from underground, united through their shared experience and their loss, they discover that the war has ended:

> They could hear the sound of birds. The trench was empty ...
> Stephen looked down to the floor of the German trench. He could not grasp what had happened. Four years that had lasted so long it seemed that time had stopped. All the men he had seen killed, their bodies, their wounds ... The tens of thousands that had gone down with him that summer morning.
> He did not know what to do. He did not know how to reclaim his life.

▶ Read the account of the opening day of the Somme in *Birdsong*. Compare it with other descriptions of the Somme that you have read. Are there any indications that this is a modern account by someone who had not been there?

By contrast with *Birdsong*, Pat Barker's trilogy of novels – *Regeneration* (1991), *The Eye in the Door* (1993) and *The Ghost Road* (1995) – approach the Great War from a very different perspective. In the first volume, the central characters are Siegfried Sassoon and the army doctor, W.H.R. Rivers, who specialised in treating officers with varying symptoms that came under the catch-all heading of shell-shock. (Rivers was as real a person as Sassoon, and Barker drew extensively on his published and unpublished papers in writing her trilogy.)

They meet at Craiglockhart Hospital, outside Edinburgh, where Sassoon was sent after making his Statement attacking the continuance of the war (see pages 30–31) in 1917. Both men are caught up in the ironies of their situation: Rivers is a scholarly and thoughtful man, who had been a social anthropologist before the war. He has to wrestle with his own conscience and sub-conscious as much as with those of his patients. He is only too aware that his job is to make men 'sane' enough again to enable them to return to the very place, the trenches, which precipitated their breakdowns in the first place. The novel's title, *Regeneration*, is thus both literal and ironic: in what sense are Rivers's patients regenerated? And for what purpose?

In the novel (as in real life) Sassoon comes quickly to realise that the only result of his protest has been to remove him to a place of greater safety, while his men (on whose behalf he had made his protest in the first place) are still confronting what he believed to be unnecessary danger at the Front. Rivers notes that the typical patient who arrived at Craiglockhart had devoted 'considerable energy to the task of forgetting whatever traumatic events had precipitated his neurosis', and Sassoon had himself recognised this in a 1917 poem 'Repression of War Experience':

> – it's bad to think of war
> When thoughts you've gagged all day come back to scare you;
> And it's been proved that soldiers don't go mad
> Unless they lose control of ugly thoughts
> That drive them out to jabber among the trees.

Rivers, in *Regeneration*, suspects that 'Sassoon's determination to remember might well account for his early and rapid recovery, though in his case it was motivated less by a desire to save his own sanity than by a determination to convince civilians that the war was mad'. Rivers' role in life, as presented in the novel, is therefore to unlock soldiers' memories of the war and in doing so he has to relive with them some of their worst nightmares. He becomes literally a father confessor to his patients, and struggles to preserve his professional detachment while doing so:

> Rivers was aware, as a constant background to his work, of a conflict between his belief that the war must be fought to a finish, for the sake of the succeeding generations, and a horror that such events … should be allowed to continue.

One of the features of Pat Barker's trilogy is that it presents the whole spectrum of attitudes to and about the war: while Rivers and Sassoon represent two faces of conscience, neither is actually a pacifist, though the second volume of the trilogy, *The Eye in the Door*, does explore the climate of radical pacifism in London during the last two years of the war. Her characters, although nearly all officers rather than rank-and-file soldiers, also cover a very broad social range: Wilfred Owen himself, whose relationship with Sassoon is one of the key elements of the story, was not from a public school background and felt his lack of social standing alongside Sassoon acutely at first. Most explicitly, the alternative hero of the novels, Billy Prior, is from a social and regional background which allows him to move across class boundaries with a confidence that the other characters cannot or do not wish to match; his bisexuality, too, gives him a freedom of movement which makes him a unique figure in writing to do with the Great War.

It is part of the achievement of the *Regeneration* trilogy (as Pat Barker's three novels have come to be known) that she is able to generate sympathy or at least respect for almost all her characters. In her exploration of the themes of memory and forgetting and of the motivations that compel her characters, she never suggests that they should be judged from a late 20th century perspective; indeed, by contrast with *Birdsong*, the novels carefully avoid adopting an historical viewpoint. And only at the end of the last chapter of the third volume, *The Ghost Road*, does Pat Barker present a set-piece battle scene as it happens rather than as it is recalled in fragments of memory grudgingly released. This is the account of the attempted crossing of the Sambre–Oise canal on 4 November 1918 ('Prompt as ever, hell erupted') and, culminating as it does in the death of Wilfred Owen, it brings the novel almost to a close. Billy Prior, already shot and dying, is the witness:

> There was no pain, more a spreading numbness that left his brain clear. He saw Kirk die. He saw Owen die, his body lifted off the ground by bullets, describing a slow arc in the air as it fell. It seemed to take forever to fall, and Prior's consciousness fluttered down with it. He gazed at his reflection in the water, which broke and reformed and broke again as the bullets hit the surface and then, gradually, as the numbness spread, he ceased to see it.

This is the most lyrical and elegiac passage (perhaps, indeed, the only one) in the entire book.

But the noise of the battle is counterpointed by another noise: at the same moment, back in London, Rivers is watching another young soldier, Hallett, dying in a hospital bed. In agony, Hallett keeps shouting out a single unintelligible word 'Shotvarfet' which drives the people around his bed , his family and fiancée, almost to distraction. Suddenly, Rivers realises what the dying man is saying:

> 'He's saying, "It's not worth it."'
> 'Oh, it is worth it, it is,' Major Hallett said, gripping his son's hand. The man was in agony. He hardly knew what he was saying.
> 'Shotvarfet.'
> The cry rose again as if he hadn't spoken, and now the other patients were growing restless. A buzz of protest not against the cry, but in support of it, a wordless murmur from damaged brains and drooping mouths.
> 'Shotvarfet. Shotvarfet.'
> 'I can't stand much more of this,' Major Hallett said. The mother's

eyes never left her son's face. Her lips were moving though she made no sound. Rivers was aware of a pressure building in his own throat as that single cry from the patients went on and on. He could not afterwards be sure that he had succeeded in keeping silent, or whether he too had joined in. All he could remember later was gripping the metal rail at the end of the bed till his hands hurt.

With this culminating scene, carefully juxtaposed with the scene of the death of Wilfred Owen, Pat Barker raises the question that runs implicitly through all writing that has dealt with the Great War. The fact that Rivers cannot later recall whether he actually joined in the hysterical chorus of 'Shotvarfet' is not an evasion: it is a recognition that the question 'Was it worth it?' is impossible to answer.

Assignments

1 Read D. H. Lawrence's essay 'With the Guns' (Part 3, pages 82–84). How do you think it would have been read by the different readers (retired soldiers, parents, men enlisting for the Army, etc.) who would have first seen it when it was published in *The Manchester Guardian*? How do you react to it today?

2 The importance of landscape and nature features prominently in much of the literature of the Great War. Examine some of the different ways writers explore this theme. Has it become more or less important in the work of later writers you have studied?

3 In what ways does the writing of the Great War period help you to understand what is meant by modernism?

4 The Great War was a central theme in the work of writers such as D.H. Lawrence, T.S. Eliot and Virginia Woolf. Research the attitudes to the war and/or to Englishness of any of these writers as expressed both in their published letters and in their fiction or poetry.

5 'The Great War has become as much a part of the mythology as of the history of the 20th century.' To what extent do you think literature has contributed to this process?

2 | Approaching the texts

- What types of texts make up the literature of the Great War?

- Is it easy to distinguish between 'literary' and 'non-literary' texts?

- How have writers used different types of material to create their own works?

- Is there a canon of Great War literature?

- Why is it important to identify when and by whom a text was written?

- Is there a mythology of the Great War?

- How does the type of text affect the way we read it?

The range of material

Probably more has been written about the Great War than about any other war in history; interest in the events of 1914–18 and in the writing generated during – and by – those four years is as intense as ever. In 1998, the eightieth anniversary of the Armistice in the United Kingdom saw a rush of new publications, newspaper articles, other journalism, exhibitions and television programmes: the public appetite for information on, and re-evaluation of, the war took even the publishers and broadcasters by surprise. It was as if, at the end of the 20th century, there was an urgent need to revisit the defining episode from its beginning.

In this revisiting, the literature of the Great War naturally played a large part: new biographies of writers such as Siegfried Sassoon were timed to coincide with the anniversary, and other publications kept alive the debate about whether or not the war poets reflected the attitudes of the ordinary population towards the war or were themselves actually opposed to war. An influential book published in 1998, *The Pity of War* by the historian Niall Ferguson (note the use of Wilfred Owen's famous phrase as the title of this book), argued that they were not.

Two other important trends became clear at this moment. First, books written about the Great War, long after it was over and by people such as Sebastian Faulks (*Birdsong*) and Pat Barker (*Regeneration, The Eye in the Door* and *The Ghost Road*) were discussed as if they were as much part of the literature of the period as those written at or just after the time. Second, the range of material that came under the heading 'literature' was suddenly much wider. Literary critics and cultural historians had been saying for a long time that the gap between fictional and non-fictional representations of the war (and indeed of any period or event in the past) was a difficult one to define. Now, however, it was possible to see how both fictional and non-fictional, 'literary' and non-'literary' writing, could serve the same purpose: bearing witness to the events of the Great War and trying to make sense of its significance.

'Literature' at its most basic means a collection of written documents, things that have been written down. 'Literary' suggests writing that is consciously (self-consciously?) concerned with style and with the emotional impact produced on the reader by the writer's creative and imaginative effort. Taking these crude definitions, a newspaper report of a battle would be part of the literature of war but not necessarily 'literary', whereas an imaginative account of it might well be both. A history book could be 'literary' as well as documentary because its style might be designed to provoke an emotional as well as an intellectual reaction from the reader. On the other hand, a novel exploring the consequences of the Great War would be literary, because it was a work of the imagination, exploiting documentary evidence to create a convincing fictional experience for the reader.

Imaginative versus documentary writing

However, the more closely these suggested definitions are examined the less convincing they seem. Even to make a basic distinction between imaginative (creative) and documentary (reported or historical) writing is to ignore the overlap between these two types of writing. Although a novel written in the 1990s must be a work of imaginative reconstruction by someone who did not live through the events he or she is writing about, such a book will draw on contemporary records and historical accounts to provide an accurate basis on which the 'authenticity' of the novel will depend. Even a book such as Edmund Blunden's *Undertones of War* (1928), written by an author who also served as a soldier in France, had to mix the factual and the imaginative. Blunden drew on his own recollections and imagination to produce a memoir 'written in Tokyo in 1924 and after, without books or papers but with the two maps I had kept, covering the regions we knew'. In the closing pages of the book Blunden describes leaving the trenches for the last time as he returned, shortly before the end of the war, to England:

> Let me look out again from the train on the way to England. We travel humbly and happily over battlefields already become historic ... houseless regions where still there are lengths of trenches twisting in and out, woods like confused ship-masts where amateur soldiers, so many of them, accepted death in lieu of war-time wages; at last we come to the old villages from which the battle of 1916 [the Somme] was begun, still rising in mutilation and in liberation. Then – not

troubling over-much about those droves of graceless tanks exercising and racing on the hill-top – we view Albert, pretty well revived, its tall chimneys smoking, its rosy roofs renewed and shining, and all about it the fields tilled, and young crops greening ... The mercy of nature advances. Is it true?

▶ In how many ways can this passage be read? What is the significance of the final question, 'Is it true?' Can the historical, literary and autobiographical strands of writing here be separated from each other? How effective is Blunden is creating a dual perspective: that of a soldier leaving the battlefields and that of an older man looking back on past experiences?

Blunden's book contained an appendix – which he called a Supplement – of poems ('Poetical Interpretations and Variations') which dealt with some of the same incidents described in prose elsewhere in *Undertones of War*. It was as if prose alone or poetry alone would not give the whole picture. This is an important point, because in a sense no one piece of writing (or whatever kind) will give the whole picture or even the essence of the picture. Every writer who revisits the Great War says (as Blunden said in the Preface to his book) 'I must go over the ground again.'

Many writers produced books about the war which, implicitly or explicitly, contain several ways of expressing or discussing the same events. *Testament of Youth* is a good example of this. It was written during the 1920s after Vera Brittain (like Edmund Blunden) had given up trying to complete a novel about the war, which she had begun while the fighting was still going on. *Testament of Youth* is essentially an autobiography, beginning with the author's birth and early childhood and ending with her marriage in 1925. Its actual construction, however, is both a **narrative** and a collage of other texts: Brittain quotes frequently from her diaries to pinpoint her thoughts and feelings at key moments in her story, and from her letters to family and friends written before, during and after the war. Many of these she quotes verbatim and at length, and it is clear that she must have asked her friends to keep her letters and to return them to her. She also quotes letters from her family, in particular from her brother Edward and from his close school friend, Roland Leighton, who was to become her fiancé. Other letters record information about events that she herself had not experienced (for instance, air-raids in England while she was nursing in Malta).

Besides these useful narrative devices, Vera Brittain also incorporates poems (mostly her own) to reflect her mood at different points in the war: often these are printed as epigraphs at the start of chapters to indicate the theme of what is to follow. Most of the poems were reproduced from her own collection of poetry, *Verses of a V.A.D.*, published in 1918. Vera Brittain had felt that this book had had too little recognition when it first appeared; reprinting much of its contents gave it a second airing. Finally, she included other documents such as the musical setting by her brother of a poem written by Roland while they were still at school.

Testament of Youth, therefore, is not simply a narrative autobiography; it has something of the feel of an album or scrapbook about it – as if the author wanted to keep every bit of evidence she could which would provide a record of the war. Like the passage from *Undertones of War* quoted above, her book has a dual perspective: it both looks back on the events of ten years before *and* it records her reactions to those events as she experienced them at the time.

Letters

This transforming of different types of texts into one larger text is characteristic of writing about the Great War. It might be thought that only poetry would avoid the tendency because it alone could be written almost spontaneously, even in the trenches. In fact, most of the poetry produced by writers such as Edward Thomas, Sassoon or Owen was not written in France: Thomas wrote letters but almost no surviving poems once he reached France; Sassoon wrote many of his poems while on sick leave in England, as did Owen, who sometimes used his letters to his mother as source material for later poems. In a letter of 4 February 1917 he described being trapped, all day, on open ground in freezing weather:

> I have no mind to describe all the horrors of this last Tour. [Owen is writing to his mother from the safety of a village where he has been billeted after the tour of duty is over, so this letter is itself a recollection of events that have passed.] But it was almost wusser than the first, because in this place my Platoon had no Dug-Outs, but had to lie in the snow under the deadly wind. By day it was impossible to stand up or even crawl about because we were behind only a little ridge screening us from the Boches' periscope.
>
> ... The marvel is that we did not all die of cold. As a matter of fact, only one of my party actually froze to death before he could be got back ... I had no real casualties from shelling, though for ten minutes every hour whizz-bangs fell a few yards short of us. Showers of soil rained on us, but no fragments of shell could find us ... We were marooned on a frozen desert.

This letter became the basis for 'Exposure', drafted in the same month, February 1917, which is one of the most poignant and powerful of all his poems:

Sudden successive flights of bullets streak the silence.
Less deathly than the air that shudders black with snow,
With sidelong flowing flakes that flock, pause, and renew;
We watch them wandering up and down the wind's nonchalance,
    But nothing happens.

Pale flakes with fingering stealth come feeling for our faces –
We cringe in holes, back on forgotten dreams, and stare,
    snow-dazed,
Deep into grassier ditches. So we drowse, sun-dozed,
Littered with blossoms trickling where the blackbird fusses,
    – Is it that we are dying?

▶ Contrast the way Owen describes the same event in the letter and in the poem: how does the poem manage to impersonalise and at the same time to universalise the experience described?

Notice the use of para-rhyme, a distinctive Owen feature, for example, snow/renew, dazed/dozed: what effect does it have on the way you read each stanza?

Astonishingly in a poem which seems to set out to expose (note the pun on the title 'Exposure') the pointlessness of the suffering endured by the soldiers, Owen actually manages to see a purpose in what they are doing – even though it is expressed in the bleakest language:

Since we believe not otherwise can kind fires burn;
Nor ever suns smile true on child, on field, or fruit.
For God's invincible spring our love is made afraid;
Therefore, not loath, we lie out here; therefore were born,
    For love of God seems dying.

By contrast, Owen's account of this episode in his letter to his mother ends more personally and perhaps more movingly:

At last I got to the village, & found all your dear precious letters, and the parcel of good and precious things. The lamp is perfect your Helmet is perfect, everything is perfect.

Letters between soldiers, their families and friends were an indispensable part of army life: the constant and prompt delivery of mail during the war was often almost miraculously kept up. Most letters were censored. Owen's duties including censoring mail from the soldiers in his company; as an officer he was able to write with a certain amount of freedom but still had to avoid giving away information about casualties, locations of troops, etc. He even invented a code which would let his mother know roughly where he was writing from. For some private soldiers, such as Isaac Rosenberg, the censorship was particularly irksome: a number of poems that he tried to send back to England were destroyed because the censoring officer said he did not have time to read 'rubbish'.

The main purpose of most letters was to reassure parents, wives, sweethearts, friends back home that their son, husband, boyfriend, etc. was still alive. Official letters from commanding officers to grieving parents or wives would explain the circumstances of a soldier's or fellow-officer's death and offer whatever comfort or consolation could be given: 'He was a very gallant officer' ... 'he was always popular with his fellow soldiers' ... 'I can assure you he will have felt very little pain' ... . Such formulae may sound like platitudes but were designed to be comforting. Siegfried Sassoon, however, exposed what he saw as this necessary hypocrisy in 'The Hero':

> 'Jack fell as he'd have wished,' the Mother said,
> And folded up the letter that she'd read.
> 'The Colonel writes so nicely.' Something broke
> In the tired voice that quavered to a choke.

Meanwhile the Brother Officer, who has been visiting Jack's mother to offer his condolences, leaves quietly:

> He'd told the poor old dear some gallant lies
> That she would nourish all her days, no doubt.

Some critics see this poem as an attack by Sassoon on women for their willingness to be taken in by such lies, and their readiness to believe that their sons' 'sacrifice' has been worthwhile; but the use of the word 'gallant' to qualify 'lies' suggests that the Brother Officer (and the Colonel) are also targets of Sassoon's satirical contempt. The final stanza reveals that Jack had actually been – in the eyes of the Brother Officer at least – a 'cold-footed, useless swine', but the ending surprisingly substitutes pathos for satire:

> at last, he died,
> Blown to small bits. And no one seemed to care
> Except that lonely woman with white hair.

Her loneliness will only be increased by the fact that she will receive no more letters, either from the Colonel or, of course, from her son.

Sometimes the letters sent from the Front presented extraordinarily detailed (and self-consciously literary) accounts of what could be seen and heard in the trenches: since soldiers were not allowed to give any military information, they concentrated on information that could be of interest to the person receiving the letter, without necessarily exposing their actual thoughts or feelings. There was a great deal that soldiers in their letters could not say, or chose not to say. Interpreting the underlying mood behind the letters is therefore often very difficult: they need to be read as carefully as any page of fiction if their ironies and omissions are to be picked up.

Ford Madox Ford (1873–1939) was a writer and critic whose novels about the Great War (especially *Parade's End*, 1924) had a great influence on other writers. In September 1916 he was – at the age of 43 – taking part in the Battle of the Somme, and sending letters daily to friends in England. Writing to the novelist Joseph Conrad on 6 September he set out to describe the sounds and emotions he was experiencing:

> In woody country heavy artillery makes most noise, because of the echoes – and most prolonged in a diluted way.
>
> On marshland – like the Romney Marsh – the sound seems alarmingly close: I have seldom heard the Hun artillery in the middle of a strafe except on marshy land. The sound, not the diluted sound, is also at its longest in the air ...
>
> Shells falling on a church: these make a huge "corump" sound, followed by a noise like crockery falling off a tray – as the roof tiles fall off. If the roof is not tiled you can hear the stained glass, sifting mechanically until the next shell. (Heard in a church square, on each occasion, about 90 yards away). Screams of women penetrate all these sounds – but I do not find that they agitate me as they have done at home. (Women in cellars round the square. Oneself running thro' fast.)

These notes on sound suggest a man who has time to write without distraction. However, in another letter, written the same day, Ford wrote to a friend called Lucy Masterman: 'We are in a h-ll of a noise just now – my hand is shaking badly – our guns are too inconsiderate ...'. The next day, 7 September, Ford wrote again to Conrad: 'I wrote these rather hurried notes yesterday because we were being shelled to hell and I did not expect to get thro' the night. I wonder if it is just vanity that in these cataclysmic moments makes one desire to record.' He then went on to suggest that Conrad might like to make use of some of the descriptions in a story of his own: 'You might want to put a phrase into the mouth of someone in Bangkok who had been, say, to Bécourt.'

It is worth noting here how what is not said can be as important as what is. To Lucy Masterman, Ford implies that the barrage of noise comes from English guns (in other words, although the noise is making his hand shake, it comes from 'friendly fire' and he is not in danger); but to Conrad, in the second letter, he admits that the shelling came from enemy fire and he thought himself likely to be killed at any moment. Astonishingly, however, he goes on in the same letter to say 'It is curious – but, in the evenings here, I always feel myself happier than I have ever felt in my life.' The emotions and attitudes described by writers when talking of their own experiences are neither predictable nor consistent.

Diaries and notebooks

Just as letters were censored, diaries and notebooks were also restricted: for this reason the most revealing diaries and notebooks from the Great War, and the most illuminating in a literary context, are often those kept by those who were non-combatant and therefore not at the Front itself. So much of the way we think of the Great War is conditioned by images of the trenches and of No Man's Land that the details of life in France and Belgium (not to mention the other theatres of war such as Mesopotamia, Italy and Palestine or, indeed, at sea) are much less well known. This is not just a matter of documentary evidence: it is as important to know what writers choose not to write about (what they decide to leave out) as to be able to imagine the situations that they do describe.

Here are two examples of entries from diaries. Each describes a situation that was certainly an important aspect of the war but which is rarely if ever mentioned in novels and poems.

> Saturday 24 November 1917, Rouen
> Visit to the Venereal Camp of 1500 men where the YMCA [Young Men's Christian Association – a religious charity working with the soldiers] Hut is in the sympathetic hands of Rev. Gilchrist (Ipswich). There are 2000 registered prostitutes in Rouen. Mr G. considers that many of these soldiers were overtaken in a fault & some are bitterly penitent. One fellow said to him 'if I were in England neither my minister nor officers would look at me & I hardly think my parents would.' Mr G. took his hand & sd. 'If Christ were here I believe this is the Camp to which He would come'. The man looked at him and turned away.

(The only novel that deals in detail with life in the Rest Camps run by the YMCA is *We That Were Young*, by Irene Rathbone, 1932. Venereal Disease was a major cause of illness and death among British troops, but is virtually undiscussed in the prose and poetry of the war. Vera Brittain briefly mentions a patient dying of syphilis in *Testament of Youth*, but on the whole it is not until the novels of the 1990s – *Birdsong* and the *Regeneration* trilogy – that the sexual activity of troops is discussed with any degree of candour. Homosexual activity was a court martial offence.)

One of the activities which the YMCA supervised was arranging visits to France by relatives of men who were thought to be dangerously ill and so could not be sent back to England. Often relatives arrived too late; if so they were allowed to stay on for the funeral. The second extract comes from the diary of an army doctor:

> After lunch today I went for a walk for some fresh air, and coming past the cemetery I saw an officer's funeral on. It was a very simple affair and yet awfully impressive. The coffin was wheeled up on a little hand-bier covered with the Union Jack, and behind it marched a firing squad of about twenty men. When they got near the grave the coffin was carried down and the soldiers formed up by the graveside while the service was read. There were two of the boy's people there, an elderly lady and a younger girl, and they stood almost alone in a little space on the other side of the grave from the soldiers' ranks.
>
> (quoted in Lyn Macdonald *The Roses of No Man's Land*)

▶ Look closely at the language and narrative style of these two diary extracts. Is it possible to say whether or not either of them is written in a 'literary' style? If so, what are the stylistic features that you identify as 'literary'? If not, how easily could you turn the material in either extract into a short story or poem written in the style of, for instance, D.H. Lawrence, Siegfried Sassoon or Susan Hill? Do these extracts help you to define more clearly what does or does not count as part of the literature of the Great War?

Songs

Some of the songs that were popular in the Great War, for instance 'It's a long, long way to Tipperary', make no particular comment on the war, and indeed belong to the traditional repertoire of marching songs popular in the Army. (It's worth remembering that the Army still did march troops over long distances in 1914–18). The songs that are more frequently cited today are those which reflected the ordinary soldiers' moods of fatalism, and apparently cheerful insubordination:

When this blasted war is over,
Oh, how happy I shall be!
When I get my civvy clothes on
No more soldiering for me.
No more church parades on Sunday,
No more asking for a pass.
I shall tell the Sergeant-Major
To stick his passes up his arse.

(Anon)

Nevertheless, songs like these became enshrined in the 1960s as part of the anti-war orthodoxy which followed the performances of Benjamin Britten's *War Requiem*, using the poetry of Wilfred Owen. In 1967 a musical revue compiled and directed by the radical London Theatre Workshop director, Joan Littlewood, became an immense popular success: entitled *Oh, What a Lovely War!*, and presenting the story of the Great War as an end of the pier show, it ridiculed Field Marshal Haig and his generals for (as the show implied) causing the unnecessary slaughter of ordinary soldiers through their own incompetence. The irony of the songs was turned into often bitter satire:

Oh, Oh, Oh it's a lovely war!
Who wouldn't be a soldier, eh?
Oh, it's a shame to take your pay.
All fours, right turn!
How shall we spend the money we earn?
Oh, Oh, Oh it's a lovely war!

This show, later turned into an even more successful film, coincided with the Peace Movement in the United States protesting against the Vietnam War. It illustrates one way in which material from the Great War itself – the songs – can later be recycled in a new literary context; and it is important to understand that, just because the songs have come to carry a strong anti-war message, this is not necessarily how they were originally seen:

Hush! Here comes a whizz-bang
And it's making straight for you …
… And you'll see all the wonders of No Man's Land
When a whizz-bang hits you!

Some of the songs of the Great War had no overt connection with the fighting at all.

One song, apparently introduced by Australian soldiers at Gallipoli in 1915, featured a notorious Sydney brothel keeper:

> Oh the moon shines bright on Mrs Porter,
> And on her daughter ...

It immediately became adopted by British troops, with additional verses replacing Mrs Porter with the comic film actor Charlie Chaplin:

> When the moon shines bright his boots are cracking
> For want of blacking,
> And his little baggy trousers want mending
> Before they send him to the Dardanelles.

Shortly after the war, this song was used in two very different literary contexts, a novel and a poem. *Tell England* (1921), a very popular and patriotic account of the Gallipoli expedition, was written by Ernest Raymond, an Anglican priest who had actually been with the British forces at Gallipoli. In a passage which may sound bizarre to a modern reader but which was meant – and taken – entirely seriously when it was first read, Raymond describes the scene on the beaches as the British soldiers wait to escape back to their ships:

> Then, about one o'clock, the moon broke the clouds and lit the operations with a white light. It should have filled us with dismay, but instead it seemed the beginning of brighter things. The men groaned merrily and burst into a drawling song:

> "Oh, the moon shines bright on Mrs Porter
> And on her daughter,
> A regular snorter;
> She has washed her neck in dirty water,
> She didn't oughter,
>   The dirty cat."

> And Monty [an army padre (chaplain), based on Raymond himself], hearing them, whispered one of his delightfully out-of-place remarks:
>   "Aren't they wonderful, Rupert? I could hug them all, but I wish they'd come to Mass."

Raymond here records the song being sung by the soldiers simply to keep their spirits up. No matter how inappropriate its subject may be, there is no intended irony in the way it is used. The following year, this song surfaced again in a much less expected place – T.S. Eliot's poem, *The Waste Land* – and here its function is more oblique. Eliot, well aware of the identity of Mrs Porter, presents a snatch of the song to counterpoint a conversation in an East End pub:

> Oh, the moon shone bright on Mrs Porter
> And on her daughter
> They wash their feet in soda water ...

The inclusion of the Australian brothel keeper, using soda water to protect herself from disease, is entirely appropriate at this moment in the poem when Eliot is evoking the sleaziness of post-war London. Again, as with the songs recycled in *Oh, What a Lovely War!*, a post-war writer is able to transform the significance of a wartime song by placing it in a different literary context.

Poetry

Of course, songs are a form of poetry but they are written to be sung or recited aloud and usually to be heard by more than one individual: their first appeal is usually to the ear rather than to the mind. Part, or even all, of the impact of a song may depend on its being sung by a group or choir together. The songs sung by soldiers on the march or relaxing in camp were important in helping to keep up morale and to reinforce the idea that war was a shared experience: the soldiers who joined in choruses such as 'We're here because we're here because we're here because we're here ...' were singing to cheer themselves and each other up as much as to make a public comment about the apparent pointlessness of what they were doing.

▶ Here are four extracts from poems written at different times and for different audiences. Some of the differences between them are clear: they look different on the page, they sound different. How easy is it, though, actually to describe and define the ways in which these pieces of writing reflect different attitudes to England, to patriotism and to experience of war and death?

> No easy hopes or lies
> Shall bring us to our goal,
> But iron sacrifice
> Of body, will, and soul.
> There is but one task for all –
> One life for each to give.
> Who stands if Freedom fall?
> Who dies if England live?
>
> (Rudyard Kipling 'For All We Have and Are')

Who'll earn the Empire's thanks –
  Will you, my laddie?
Who'll swell the victor's ranks –
  Will you, my laddie?
When that procession comes,
Banners and rolling drums –
Who'll stand and bite his thumbs –
  Will you, my laddie?

(Jessie Pope 'The Call')

When you see millions of the mouthless dead
Across your dreams in pale battalions go,
Say not soft things as other men have said,
That you'll remember, for you need not so.
Give them not praise. For, deaf, how should they know
It is not curses heaped on each gashed head?
Nor tears. Their blind eyes see not your tears flow.
Nor honour. It is easy to be dead.

(Charles Hamilton Sorley 'Sonnet')

Rest at last and no danger for another week, a seven-day week.
But one Private took on himself a Company's heart to speak,
'I wish to bloody hell I was just going to Brewery – surely
To work all day (in Stroud) and be free at tea-time – allowed
Resting when one wanted, and a joke in season.
To change clothes and take a girl to Horsepool's turning,
Or drink a pint at "Travellers Rest", and find no cloud.
Then God and man and war and Gloucestershire would have a reason,
But I get no good in France, getting killed, cleaning off mud.'
He spoke the heart of all of us – the hidden thought burning, unturning.

(Ivor Gurney 'Billet')

As with the fiction and memoirs of the Great War, much of the poetry was written
long after the conflict was over, and indeed specifically looks back at it from an
historical perspective. So it is important to identify when a poem was written, as
well as by whom: whether combatant or non-combatant. It is also important to ask
whether the writer is trying to recreate the immediacy of an experience that took
place in the past or whether he or she is trying to see it in an historical context, to
see the Great War as part of the continuum of war. The Welsh poet and artist David
Jones was very conscious of the way in which the Great War was both like and
unlike previous wars. In the Preface to *In Parenthesis* (1937) he compared the
experience of soldiers saying farewell in 1915 with that of Shakespeare's foot-
soldiers in *Henry V*:

We are in no doubt at all but what Bardolph's marching kiss for Pistol's 'quondam Quickly' is an experience substantially the same as you and I suffered on Victoria platform. For the old authors there appears to have been no such dilemma – for them the embrace of battle seemed to have been one with the embrace of lovers. For us it is different … I only wish to record that for me such a dilemma exists, and that I have been particularly conscious of it during the making of this writing.

In his poem, Jones combines prose and verse, historical and literary reference, army jargon with cockney slang, and Welsh vernacular with the devotional idiom of Catholic prayers. He does this in a form of linguistic collage, like a picture in words to show both the mixture of men fighting alongside each other and the sense in which what is happening to these men in battle is both the same as, and different from, what has happened in past wars. In the passage printed in Part 3 (pages 80–81), he describes the attempt to carry a badly wounded man away from the battlefield while his companions remain under attack.

▶ How many different types of speech or voice can you identify in this passage? How effectively does the way the writing is put together convey the confusion of the scene and the variety of thoughts and feelings? Try to define as many ways as possible (no matter how obvious they appear at first) in which this writing differs from other war poetry you have read. On what grounds could you call *In Parenthesis* modernist in style and impact?

Fiction

Like the poetry generated by the Great War, so with prose fiction: much that is written and said about the novels of the Great War refers only to a very small number of books. For this reason, the publication in the 1990s of novels such as Sebastian Faulks' *Birdsong* and Pat Barker's *Regeneration* trilogy has significantly extended the range of Great War prose fiction. It is also important to note that two of the most influential novels of the Great War were not written in English. The first of these (indeed one of the first of all the war novels) was by a Frenchman, Henri Barbusse. *Le Feu* was originally published in serial form (monthly episodes in a magazine called *L'Oeuvre* – a way of publishing fiction that had been popular in the 19th century) from August 1916 onwards and then as a full-length novel in 1917. Remarkably, for a book published while the war was barely half over, Barbusse was able to offer an apocalyptic vision of the world transformed for ever by war. The conditions and suffering endured in this war, Barbusse argued, were so extreme that people should never, and must never, be forced to endure them again.

A recent critic, Jay Winter, has described Barbusse as 'a modern Noah, who has been through the Flood, and demanded a new covenant, a new order, an order without war':

> *Le Feu* offered a message of hope. This is what helped to give his book its massive appeal and power. It spoke to the bereaved as much to the soldiers with whom Barbusse had served. One teacher from the Ardèche, aged twenty, had lost her husband in the War. She wrote to Barbusse to thank him for his book and for his message of hope. She 'took courage to think that those who died did not die in vain – if the present cataclysm produces a modification of human destiny'. 'One can't remake life', Barbusse mused, 'but one can avoid death' in future. It was this task, the avoidance of the calamity of war, which Barbusse was to make his life's work.
>
> (*Sites of Memory, Sites of Mourning*, 1995)

Avoiding the calamity of war was the task that other writers of fiction – and of prose memoirs and poetry – also set themselves in the period between the two World Wars. No writer presented his case more poignantly than the German novelist Erich Maria Remarque, whose novel *All Quiet on the Western Front* was published in English translation in 1929. This novel, which later became a very influential film, emphasised the pity of war rather than the anger of it. The central characters, a group of friends who enlist together and experience the reality of life and death in the trenches, are shown being drawn closer and closer together as they feel themselves more and more cut off from those at home. It is very significant that this book appeared at the same time as the majority of English prose works and that, though written by a German from a German perspective, its message has always been read as a universal, or at least a European, one.

Not all novels dealing with the Great War, however, have taken this theme. One of the most popular, *Tell England* by Ernest Raymond (1921), was written to celebrate the patriotic commitment of those who had fought and died. It was also a book which did much to fix in the public's mind the connection between the English public schools, with their muscular Christianity and military training (see also the early chapters of Vera Brittain's *Testament of Youth*) and the idea of the cheerful sacrifice of youth – though only of the officer class, 'other ranks' are conspicuously absent in the book.

▶ Read again the extract from *Tell England* on page 64. How do you think readers in 1921 might have responded to this passage? How do you respond to it yourself? Do you think that modern readers bring a sense of irony to their reading which would have puzzled earlier readers?

The 'myth' of the Great War and the Great War in modern mythology

At the very least *Tell England*, with its open enthusiasm for the war in its final stages, is a useful reminder that the mood in Britain at the end of the war was not entirely of gloom, disillusionment and exhaustion. Those emotions tended to be expressed (in prose if not in poetry) later on, and there is always the danger of reading back into a piece of writing attitudes which it did not originally contain, or intend to express. The critic Samuel Hynes, who has written two important books about the cultural history of war in the 20th century (*A War Imagined* and *The Soldiers' Tale*) has defined what he calls the 'myth' of the Great War in these terms:

> ... a generation of innocent young men, their heads full of high abstractions like Honour, Glory and England, went off to war to make the world safe for democracy. They were slaughtered in stupid battles planned by stupid generals. Those who survived were shocked, disillusioned and embittered by their war experiences, and saw that their real enemies were not the Germans, but the old men at home who had lied to them. They rejected the values of the society that had sent them to war, and in doing so separated their own generation from the past and from their cultural inheritance.
>
> *(The Soldiers' Tale)*

Hynes points out that this myth did not become common until the mid-1920s, and he accounts for it 'partly as the product of an emerging awareness, as the post-war years passed, that the war had brought nothing about; and partly as a kind of leakage from war poetry and fiction, the more emotive forms for re-creating experience'.

▶ Read the extract from Richard Aldington's 'Farewell to Memories' (Part 3, pages 73–74). When do you think the short story from which this passage comes might have been written? How would you sum up the attitude to the war, and its aftermath, expressed in this passage? What effect do you think is achieved in this passage by contrasting third and first person narratives? Contrast the style and mood with the extract from *Undertones of War* on pages 55–56.

It is clear that not all the writers who produced books and poetry in the post-war decade up to 1929 saw themselves as writing anti-war books. Robert Graves claimed to have been surprised by the critics who described *Goodbye to All That* as 'a violent treatise against war' and said that he had tried 'not to show any bias for or against war as a human institution' (quoted by Hynes in *The Soldiers' Tale*), and

Edmund Blunden claimed that *Undertones of War* had been written as 'the record of a happy battalion'. Were they telling the truth about their intentions? Or were they unaware of what they were actually writing? Had Graves forgotten that he had already published such a poem as 'A Dead Boche' which described itself as offering 'a certain cure' for anyone who thought war was a noble or glorious affair? Had Blunden not realised the impact of the poems he himself added as a supplement to his prose memoir? It is important to remember that writers, like anyone else, can say different things at different times and that – even if these things seem contradictory – this may not always be so. The myth of the Great War, and the evidence for and against it, is much more complex than first appears.

A canon of Great War literature?

- What are the essential literary texts that define the significance of the Great War in the cultural history of the 20th century?

- Who decides which texts are essential, and on what grounds?

- Would different lists of 'essential' texts define the significance of the Great War in different ways?

First, it must be remembered that there is a difference between literature that emerged directly from the Great War, either written only by those who fought in it (in other words, men and not women) or by those who lived through it without actually fighting, and literature written subsequently by those not even alive during 1914–18. Then there is also literature which does not treat the war as its main subject but in which the war plays a significant part. Again, there is literature which is not self-consciously 'literary' – letters, diaries, etc. – but which may have a right to be considered part of the canon. Reviewers and publishers are keen to describe new titles as 'a significant addition to the canon', both as a way of claiming a certain status for the book and (perhaps) of boosting its sales.

For much of the 20th century, the canon of Great War literature was limited to the 'trench poets' and to a few novels. The idea that women could contribute to this canon was barely considered. Novels such as *The Return of the Soldier* (1918) by 'serious' writers – but what are 'serious' as opposed to non-serious writers? – like Rebecca West did not count because she had not physically participated in the war. The token woman allowed in the canon was Vera Brittain, both because *Testament of Youth* fitted the prevailing mood of opposition to war and because she had at least been a nurse if she couldn't be a soldier. Other writing by women (for instance, the novel *We That Were Young*, by Irene Rathbone, 1932) enjoyed a certain popularity but did not survive in print. Is that a definition of canonical – a book that stays in print so long that it is almost bound to remain in print regardless of fashion? It is hard to imagine that Wilfred Owen's poetry or Siegfried Sassoon's *Memoirs of an Infantry Officer* will ever go out of print now, but has a poet like Ivor Gurney at last become canonical? T.S. Eliot described David Jones' *In Parenthesis* as 'a work of genius'; is that sufficient to justify its place in the canon? Will Pat Barker's *Regeneration* really become part of the canon? Has *Tell England* by Ernest Raymond fallen so far out of fashion and print that it can no longer be thought of as part of the canon? Or did the fact that this novel celebrated a 'just' war rather than condemned it mean that it could never have been part of the canon anyway?

The idea of canons in literature (and still more, of a canon of literature as a whole) has become problematic. As all the questions in the previous paragraphs imply, there is little agreement about what the canon of Great War literature should contain, and even about whether lists of books in themselves are particularly helpful. When one book is 'privileged' at the expense of another, it is important to ask what that choice says about the two books (and about the attitude of the people who make the choice) in literary, cultural or historical terms.

Assignments

1   Working within a group, or on your own, try to decide what rules you would lay down for establishing a canon of texts to represent the Great War in British literature. If you find some of your rules contradict each other (for example, 'novels directly about the Great War' and 'only texts written by those who were alive during 1914–18), try to divide your rules into two sets, and sketch two, or more, different lists of Great War texts. Then, ask what picture of the war and its significance for British culture in the 20th century each list provides. What part do you think fashion – political, literary or otherwise – plays in helping to define the canon?

2   D.H. Lawrence's essay 'With the Guns' (Part 3, pages 82–84) was originally written as a newspaper article. On what grounds would you include or exclude it as part of the canon of Great War literature?

3   Look at the account of the death of Wilfred Owen from Jon Stallworthy's biography (Part 3, page 94) and compare it with the account of the same episode in Pat Barker's *The Ghost Road* (page 76). Should the fact that the first is biography while the second is fiction exclude it from consideration as part of the canon, in your view, or not? Think carefully about the reasons for your answer to this question.

4 How easy is it to distinguish between 'literary' and 'documentary' writing about the Great War?

5 Write a short story, extract of a novel or poem(s) in the style of any Great War writer whose work you have encountered. Then reflect on what this has shown you about the way the original writer approached the problems of writing during (or after) and about the Great War. It may help you to take as a starting point letters, pictures, souvenirs or artefacts from the Great War that you have read, seen in a museum or gallery or still possess in your family.

3 | Texts and extracts

The texts and extracts that follow have been chosen to illustrate key themes and points made elsewhere in the book, and to provide material which may be useful when working on the assignments in Parts 1, 2, 4 and 5. As far as possible, space has been given to texts and extracts which are not so readily available elsewhere rather than to poems and prose which can easily be found in anthologies or other editions. For this reason there is an emphasis on work written and published in the aftermath of the Great War. The items are arranged alphabetically by author.

Richard Aldington (1892–1962)

From 'Farewell to Memories' (published by Aldington as the last in a collection of short stories, *Roads to Glory*, 1930), and 'In Memory of Wilfred Owen' (1931)

The title of the story is significant, with its explicit statement that the speaker is taking leave, not just of the war, but of the memories that have stayed with him for more than a decade since the Armistice.

Aldington's poem addresses Owen as the representative of all who gave 'all you had, to forget'. Aldington and Owen never met, but both were involved in the fighting on the Western Front in the latter part of the war.

> The train which was taking Brandon back to England for the last time started from Cambrai before dawn. About eight miles from the town, in the Somme battle-field, it halted for nearly two hours. Brandon stared out the window, still wearing his full equipment, with his rifle mechanically clutched between his knees. The colourless winter dawn hovered mournfully over a desecrated land, over a wreckage and sorrow that were beyond tears or outcries. Nothing can express that pitiable frozen silence, that awful symbol of the hatred of men for men. There stood a broken tank, poised on the verge of a huge shell-hole, just as it met disaster months before. There still lay the debris of battle. Guns, cocked sideways on broken wheels, showed where the men had died. The frozen landscape was a tumult of shell-holes. Everywhere stood little groups of crosses; and to the south was a large, neatly lined cemetery. That was the symbol of the youth of a generation – line of crosses. That was the symbol for all of them, living or dead – a graveyard on a battle-field. Never again would there be hope and gladness, never again free laughter and the joy of a girl's soft lips. Through the music and the laughter, through the soft touches and the voice of desire and the starry eyes, always, always they would see that silent landscape, always see the lines of humble

crosses marking a world destroyed. Men passed his window, going to the engine to beg a little boiling water to make tea. Brandon scarcely saw them. With the tears trickling slowly down his cheeks, he saw only the lines upon lines upon lines of crosses. There was no room for bitterness even, no need for speech.

We pass and leave you lying. No need for rhetoric, for funeral music for melancholy bugle-calls. No need for tears now, no need for regret.

We took our risk with you; you died and we live. We take your noble gift, salute for the last time those lines of pitiable crosses, those solitary mounds, those unknown graves, and turn to live our lives out as we may.

Which of us were fortunate – who can tell? For you there is silence and the cold twilight drooping in awful desolation over those motionless lands. For us sunlight and the sound of women's voices, song and hope and laughter, despair, gaiety, love – life.

Lost terrible silent comrades, we, who might have died, salute you.

In Memory of Wilfred Owen
I had half-forgotten among the soft blue waters
And the gay-fruited arbutus of the hill
Where never the nightingales are silent,
And the sunny hours are warm with honey and dew;

I had half-forgotten as the stars slid westward
Year after year in grave majestic order,
In the strivings and in the triumphs of manhood,
The world's voice, and the touch of beloved hands.

But I have never quite forgotten, never forgotten
All you who lie there so lonely, and never stir
When the hired buglers call unheeded to you,
Whom the sun shall never warm nor the frost chill.

Do you remember ... but why should you remember?
Have you not given all you had, to forget?
Oh, blessed, blessed be Death! They can no more vex you,
You for whom memory and forgetfulness are one.

Marian Allen

These two sonnets were first published in *The Wind on the Downs* (1918). About the author no information has survived, but some of her poems were reprinted in *Scars Upon My Heart* (1981).

The Wind on the Downs

I'd meant to write to you about the Downs,
And of the white chalk roads that stretch away
To distant views of huddled Sussex towns
And windmills standing sentinel and grey.
I'd meant to climb until I saw the sea,
The channel like a silver ribbon shine;
And feel the Down wind blowing strong and free,
And hear the guns from the far battle-line.
Again I stand upon the wind-swept grass,
Six months ago so stilled and white with frost;
Since then your strange adventure came to pass,
For as I wander on the Downs I see
Your shadow in the wind chase after me.

Charing Cross

I went along the river-side to-day
Under the railway bridge at Charing Cross,
Where many such as you are sped away
And we are left to wonder at your loss.
The station echoes with your ghostly feet;
Your laughing voices cling about each wall;
You entered gaily from the sunlit street
To pass into the sun again and fall.
The train slid out under the April sky,
And London's throbbing heart was left behind;
And many more will follow you to die,
Crossing the silent river, there to find
Host upon host their comrades glorified,
Saluting them upon the other side.

Pat Barker (1943–)

From *The Ghost Road* (1995)

This passage, from very near the end of the last book in Pat Barker's *Regeneration* trilogy, sets the death of Wilfred Owen alongside the fictional hero of the novel, Billy Prior. Owen was killed on 4 November 1918 during the crossing of the Sambre-Oise Canal.

Bridges laid down, quickly, efficiently, no bunching at the crossings, just the clump of boots on wood, and then they emerged from beneath the shelter of the trees and out into the terrifying openness of the bank. As bare as an eyeball, no cover anywhere, and the machine-gunners on the other side were alive and well. They dropped down, firing to cover the sappers as they struggled to assemble the bridge, but nothing covered them. Bullets fell like rain, puckering the surface of the canal, and the men started to fall. Prior saw the man next to him, a silent, surprised face, no sound, as he twirled and fell, a slash of scarlet like a huge flower bursting open on his chest. Crawling forward, he fired at the bank opposite though he could hardly see it for the clouds of smoke that drifted across. The sappers were still struggling with the bridge, binding pontoon sections together with wire that sparked in their hands as bullets struck it. And still the terrible rain fell. Only two sappers left, and then the Manchesters took over the building of the bridge. Kirk paddled out in a crate to give covering fire, was hit, hit again, this time in the face, went on firing directly at the machine-gunners who crouched in their defended holes only a few yards away. Prior was about to start across the water with ammunition when he was himself hit, though it didn't feel like a bullet, more like a blow from something big and hard, a truncheon or a cricket bat, only it knocked him off his feet and he fell, one arm trailing over the edge of the canal.

He tried to turn to crawl back beyond the drainage ditches, knowing it was only a matter of time before he was hit again, but the gas was thick here and he couldn't reach his mask. Banal, simple, repetitive thoughts ran round and round his mind. *Balls up. Bloody mad. Oh Christ.* There was no pain, more a spreading numbness that left his brain clear. He saw Kirk die. He saw Owen die, his body lifted off the ground by bullets, describing a slow arc in the air as it fell. It seemed to take for ever to fall, and Prior's consciousness fluttered down with it. He gazed at his reflection in the water, which broke and reformed and broke again as bullets hit the surface and then, gradually, as the numbness spread, he ceased to see it.

Edmund Blunden (1896–1974)

These poems by Blunden were written in the shadow of the approaching Second World War: 'To W.O. and His Kind' appeared in 1939 and 'To Wilfred Owen' in 1940.

To W.O. and His Kind

If even you, so able and so keen,
And master of the business you reported
Seem now almost as though you had never been,
And in your simple purpose nearly thwarted,
What hope is there? What harvest from those hours
Deliberately, and in the name of truth,
Endured by you? Your witness moves no Powers,
And younger youth resents your sentient youth.

You would have stayed me with some parable,
The grain of mustard seed, the boy that thrust
His arm into the leaking dike to quell
The North Sea's onrush. Would you were not dust.
With you I might invent, and make men try,
Some genuine shelter from this frantic sky.

To Wilfred Owen
Killed in action November 4th, 1918

Where does your spirit walk, kind soldier, now,
In this deep winter, bright with ready guns?
And have you found new poems in this war?

Some would more wish you, with untroubled brow,
Perpetual sleep, which you perhaps wished once –
To unknow this swift return of all you bore.

And yet, if ever in the scheme of things
Past men have leave to see the world they loved,
This night you crossed the lines, for a second seen

By worried sentries. In vast tunnellings
You track the working-party; by the gloved
Wire-sergeant stand; look in at the canteen;

And I, dream-following you, reading your eyes,
Your veteran youthful eyes, discover fair
Some further hope, which did not formerly rise.
Smiling you fade, the future meets you there.

Vera Brittain (1893–1970)

From *Testament of Youth* (1933)

This passage illustrates Brittain's use of her diary and of letters from her brother Edward to compile her narrative. Roland [Leighton], her fiancé, had been killed just before Christmas in 1915.

"I wonder," I wrote in my diary after the first afternoon under a new Charge-Sister in my old sixty-bed hut, "if ever, ever I shall get over this feeling of blank hopelessness ... Resistance requires an energy which I haven't any of – and to try to acquire it just to face bravely a world that has ceased to interest me ... hardly seems worth while."

It was just at this moment that Edward wrote to say that his orders to go to the front had come at last and he was leaving London for France on February 10th. The date was memorable for other reasons, since it brought conscription into operation in England for the first time in history, but about this I neither knew nor cared when my mother and I saw him off from Charing Cross on one of those grey, unutterably dismal afternoons in which a London February seems to specialise. With him went two other officers who were also joining the 11th Sherwood Foresters – the one, Captain H., a big bluff, friendly man who afterwards became his company commander; the other a plump insignificant subaltern who live long enough to find death and presumably glory in the final advance on the Western front.

As I dragged myself back to Camberwell my feet seemed weighted with lead, and I realised that there had still, after all, been something capable of increasing the misery of the past few weeks.

"I cannot cherish any optimistic hopes about the front now ..." my diary recorded. "Yet I cannot feel very acutely – I don't feel anything but an utter, utter weariness. ... It is all so unbelievable. He – to be standing in water and mud, when I can remember him in a brown holland overall, and everyone was always so careful to see that he didn't get his feet wet ... I do not think about him in the same invariable way as I thought and think about Roland. But when I do think about him, which is very often indeed, I realise how it is to him all my hopes of the future are anchored, upon him that my chances of companionship and understanding in the future depend."

A week later a letter came to say that he was already in the trenches.

"It is quite easy for me now," he wrote, "to understand how Roland was killed; it was quite ordinary but just unlucky ... I do not hold life cheap at all and it is hard to be sufficiently brave, yet I have hardly ever felt really afraid. One has to keep up appearances at all costs even if one does."

John Drinkwater (1882–1937)

From *x = o: An Incident of the Trojan War* (1917)

This play was one of the first to comment on the wastefulness and futility of war, and could only do so on the open stage by being set in the Trojan War.

> *On Troy Wall. CAPYS, a young Trojan soldier, is on guard, looking out over the plain where the Greeks are encamped. ILUS, another young soldier, his friend, wearing a bearskin, comes to him.*

ILUS   When does your watch end?

CAPYS   In two hours; at midnight.

ILUS   They're beautiful, those tents, under the star.
It is my night to go like a shadow among them,
And, snatching a Greek life, come like a shadow again.
It's an odd skill to have won in the rose of your youth –
Two years, and once in every seven days – a hundred.
More than a hundred, and only once a fault.
A hundred Greek boys, Capys, like myself –
Loving, and quick in honour, and clean of fear –
Spoiled in their beauty by me whose desire is beauty
Since I first walked the April hedgerows. Would time
But work upon this Helen's face, maybe
This nine-year quarrel would be done, and Troy
Grow sane, and her confounding councillors
Be given carts to clean and drive to market
What of your sea-girl? Has she grown?

CAPYS   You ask
Always the question, friend. The chisels rust,
The moths are in my linen coats, my mallets
Are broken. Ilus, in my brain were limbs
Supple and mighty; the beauty of women moved
To miraculous birth in my imagining;
I had conceived the body of man, to make
Divine articulation of the joy
That flows uncounted in every happy step
Of health; the folk faring about Troy streets
Should have flowered upon my marble marvellously:
I would have given my land a revelation
Sweet as the making of it had been to me.
And still it shall be, if ever from my mind
Falls this obscure monotony, that makes
The world an echo, its vivid gesture gone.
Troy peaceful shall be Troy magnificent,
For I will make her so.

Ivor Gurney (1890–1937)

Gurney was both a composer and a poet, who served as a private soldier in France with his local regiment, the Gloucesters. After the war, he spent the final years of his life in a mental asylum. His poetry was first edited by Edmund Blunden. 'The Silent One' was first published in 1922.

The Silent One

Who died on the wires, and hung there, one of two –
Who for his hours of life had chattered through
Infinite lovely chatter of Bucks accent;
Yet faced unbroken wires; stepped over, and went,
A noble fool, faithful to his stripes – and ended.
But I weak, hungry, and willing only for the chance
Of line – to fight in the line, lay down under unbroken
Wires, and saw the flashes, and kept unshaken.
Till the politest voice – a finicking accent, said:
'Do you think you might crawl through, there; there's a hole:' In
　the afraid
Darkness, shot at; I smiled, as politely replied –
'I'm afraid not, Sir.' There was no hole, no way to be seen.
Nothing but chance of death, after tearing of clothes.
Kept flat, and watched the darkness, hearing bullets whizzing –
And thought of music – and swore deep heart's deep oaths
(Polite to God –) and retreated and came on again,
Again retreated – and a second time faced the screen.

David Jones (1895–1974)

From *In Parenthesis* (1937)

Critics are divided over whether *In Parenthesis* supports or challenges the view that the Great War is a 20th century rewriting of the wars of the past. T.S. Eliot praised the poem as a work of genius, and it is one of the most unusual and important works in the canon of Great War literature.

Nothing is impossible nowadays my dear if only we can get the poor
bleeder through the barrage and they take just as much trouble with
the ordinary soldiers you know and essential-service academicians
can match the natural hue and everything extraordinarily well.
　Give them glass eyes to see
and synthetic spare parts to walk in the Triumphs, without anyone
feeling awkward and O, O, O, its a lovely war with poppies on the up-

platform for a perpetual memorial of his body.
Lift gently Dai, gentleness befits his gun-shot wound in the lower
bowel – go easy – easee at the slope – and mind him – wait for this
one and
slippy – an' twelve inch an' all – beating up for his counter-attack and
– that packet on the Aid-Post.
   Lower you lower you – some old cows have malhandled little
bleeders for a mother's son.
   Lower you lower you prize Maria Hunt, an' gammyfingered upland
Gamalin – down cantcher – low – hands away me ducky – down on
hands on hands down and flattened belly and face pressed and
curroodle mother earth
she's kind:
Pray her hide you in her deeps
she's only refuge against
this ferocious pursuer
terribly questing.
Maiden of the digged places
                          let our cry come unto thee.
Mam, moder, mother of me
Mother of Christ under the tree
reduce our dimensional vulnerability to the minimum –
cover the spines of us
let us creep back dark-bellied where he can't see
don't let it.
There, there, it can't, won't hurt – nothing
shall harm my beautiful.
   But on its screaming passage
their numbers writ
and stout canvas tatters drop as if they'd salvoed grape to the
mizzen-sheets and the shaped ash grip rocket-sticks out of
the evening sky right back by Bright Trench
and clots and a twisted clout
on the bowed back of the F.O.O. bent to his instrument.

D.H. Lawrence (1885–1930)

This essay was first published in *The Manchester Guardian* on 18 August 1914. It shows Lawrence's remarkable insight, almost before the war has begun, into the nature of modern warfare.

With the Guns

The Reservists were leaving for London by the nine o'clock train. They were young men, some of them drunk. There was one bawling and brawling before the ticket window; there were two swaying on the steps of the subway shouting, and ending, "Let's go an' have another afore we go." There were a few women seeing off their sweethearts and brothers, but, on the whole, the reservist had been a lodger in the town and had only his own pals. One woman stood before the carriage window. She and her sweetheart were being very matter-of-fact, cheerful, and bumptious over the parting.

"Well, so-long!" she cried as the train began to move. "When you see 'em let 'em have it."

"Ay, no fear," shouted the man, and the train was gone, the man grinning.

I thought what it would really be like, "when he saw 'em."

*　　*　　*　　*　　*　　*　　*　　*

Last autumn I followed the Bavarian army down the Isar valley and near the foot of the Alps. Then I could see what war would be like – an affair entirely of machines, with men attached to the machines as the subordinate part thereof, as the butt is the part of a rifle.

I remember standing on a little round hill one August afternoon. There was a beautiful blue sky, and white clouds from the mountains. Away on the right, amid woods and corn-clad hills, lay the big Starnberg lake. This is just a year ago, but it seems to belong to some period outside of time.

On the crown of the little hill were three quick-firing guns, with the gunners behind. At the side, perched up on a tiny platform at the top of a high pair of steps, was an officer looking through a fixed spy-glass. A little further behind, lower down the hill, was a group of horses and soldiers.

Every moment came the hard, tearing hideous voice of the German command from the officer perched aloft, giving the range to the guns; and then the sharp cry, "Fire!" There was a burst, something in the guns started back, the faintest breath of vapour disappeared. The shots had gone.

I watched, but I could not see where they had gone, nor what had

been aimed at. Evidently they were directed against an enemy a mile and a half away, men unseen by any of the soldiers at the guns. Whether the shot they fired hit or missed, killed or did not touch, I and the gun-party did not know. Only the officer was shouting the range again, the guns were again starting back, we were again staring over the face of the green and dappled, inscrutable country into which the missiles sped unseen.

What work was there to do? – only mechanically to adjust the guns and fire the shot. What was there to feel? – only the unnatural suspense and suppression of serving a machine which, for aught we knew, was killing our fellow-men, whilst we stood there, blind, without knowledge or participation, subordinate to the cold machine. This was the glamour and the glory of the war: blue sky overhead and living green country all around, but we, amid it all, a part in some iron insensate will, our flesh and blood, our soul and intelligence shed away, and all that remained of us a cold, metallic adherence to an iron machine. There was neither ferocity nor joy nor exultation nor exhilaration nor even quick fear: only a mechanical, expressionless movement.

And this is how the gunner would "let 'em have it." He would mechanically move a certain apparatus when he heard a certain shout. Of the result he would see and know nothing. He had nothing to do with it.

Then I remember going at night down a road, whilst the sound of guns thudded continuously. And suddenly I started, seeing the bank of the road stir. It was a mass of scarcely visible forms, lying waiting for a rush. They were lying under fire, silent, scarcely stirring, a mass. If one of the shells that were supposed to be coming had dropped among them it would have burst a hole in the mass. Who would have been torn, killed, no one would have known. There would just have been a hole in the living shadowy mass; that was all. Who it was did not matter. There were no individuals, and every individual soldier knew it. He was a fragment of a mass, and as a fragment of a mass he must live and die or be torn. He had no rights, no self, no being. There was only the mass lying there, solid and obscure along the bank of the road in the night.

This was how the gunner "would let 'em have it." A shell would fall into this mass of vulnerable bodies, there would be a torn hole in the mass. This would be his "letting 'em have it".

And I remember a captain of the bersaglieri who talked to me in the train in Italy when he had come back from Tripoli. The Italian soldier, he said, was the finest soldier in the world at a rush. But – and he spoke with a certain horror that cramped his voice – when it came

to lying there under the Snyder fire you had to stand behind them with a revolver. And I saw he could not get beyond the agony of this.

"Well," I said, "that is because they cannot feel themselves parts of a machine. They have all the old natural courage, when one rushes at one's enemy. But it is unnatural to them to lie still under machine-fire. It is unnatural to anybody. War with machines, and the machine predominant, is too unnatural for an Italian. It is a wicked thing a machine, and your Italians are too naturally good. They will do anything to get away from it. Let us see our enemy and go for him. But we cannot endure this taking death out of machines, and giving death out of machines, our blood cold, without any enemy to rise against."

I remember also standing on a little hill crowned by a white church. This hill was defended, surrounded by a trench half-way down. In this trench stood the soldiers side by side, down there in the earth, a great line of them.

The night came on. Suddenly, on the other side, high up in the darkness, burst a beautiful greenish globe of light, and then came into being a magic circle of countryside set in darkness, a greenish jewel of landscape, splendid bulk of trees, a green meadow, vivid. The ball fell and it was dark, and in one's eye remained treasured the little vision that had appeared far off in the darkness. Then again a light ball burst and sloped down. There was the white farm house with the wooden, slanting roof, the green apple trees, the orchard paling, a jewel, a landscape set deep in the darkness. It was beautiful beyond belief. Then it was dark. Then the searchlights suddenly sprang upon the countryside, revealing the magic, fingering everything with magic, pushing the darkness aside, showing the lovely hillsides, the sable bulks of trees, the pallor of corn. A searchlight was creeping at us. It slid up our hill. It was upon us; we turned out backs to it, it was unendurable. Then it was gone.

Then out of a little wood at the foot of the hill came the intolerable crackling and bursting of rifles. The men in the trenches returned fire. Nothing could be seen. I thought of the bullets that would find their marks. But whose bullets? And what mark. Why must I fire off my gun in the darkness towards a noise? Why must a bullet come out of the darkness, breaking a hole in me? But better a bullet than the laceration of a shell, if it came to dying. But what is it all about? I cannot understand; I am not to understand. My God, why am I a man at all, when this is all, this machinery piercing and tearing?

It is a war of artillery, a war of machines, and men no more than the subjective material of the machine. It is so unnatural as to be unthinkable. Yet we must think of it.

W. Somerset Maugham (1874–1965)

From *For Services Rendered* (1932)

In this passage from the play, Mr Ardsley is faced with two conflicting responses to the war from two veterans, his son Sydney and his son-in-law Howard. The play appeared at a time when several books by survivors of the Great War had started to challenge whether anything had actually been achieved or learned in the decade that had followed the signing of the Treaty of Versailles in 1919.

SYDNEY   *(with bitter calm)* You see, I feel I have a certain right to speak. I know how dead keen we all were when the war started. Every sacrifice was worth it. We didn't say much about it because we were rather shy, but honour did mean something to us and patriotism wasn't just a word. And then, when it was all over, we did think that those of us who'd died hadn't died in vain, and those of us who were broken and shattered and knew they wouldn't be any more good in the world were buoyed up by the thought that if they'd given everything they'd given it in a great cause.

ARDSLEY   And they had.

SYDNEY   Do you still think that? I don't. I know that we were the dupes of the incompetent fools who ruled the nations. I know that we were sacrificed to their vanity, their greed, and their stupidity. And the worst of it is that as far as I can tell they haven't learnt a thing. They're just as vain, they're just as greedy, they're just as stupid as they ever were. They muddle on, muddle on, and one of these days they'll muddle us all into another war. When that happens I'll tell you what I'm going to do. I'm going out into the streets and cry: 'Look at me, don't be a lot of damned fools; it's all bunk what they're saying to you, about honour and patriotism and glory. Bunk, bunk, bunk.

HOWARD   Who cares if it is bunk? I had the time of my life in the war. No responsibility and plenty of money. More than I'd ever had before or ever since. All the girls you wanted and all the whisky. Excitement. A roughish time in the trenches, but a grand lark afterwards. I tell you it was a bitter day for me when they signed the armistice. What have I got now? Just the same old thing day after

	day, working my guts out to keep body and soul together. The very day war is declared I join up and the sooner the better, if you ask me. That's the life for me. By God!
ARDSLEY	*(to his son)* You've had a lot to put up with, Sydney. I know that. But don't think you're the only one. It's been a great blow to me that you haven't been able to follow me in my business as I followed my father. Three generations, that would have been. But it wasn't to be. No one wants another war less than I do, but if it comes I'm convinced that you'll do your duty, so far as in you lies, as you did it before. It was a great grief to me that when the call came I was too old to answer. But I did what I could. I was enrolled as a special constable. And if I'm wanted again I shall be ready again.
SYDNEY	*(between his teeth)* God give me patience.
HOWARD	You have a whisky and soda, old boy, and you'll feel better.

Charlotte Mew (1869–1928)

The Cenotaph, designed by the architect Sir Edwin Lutyens and erected in Whitehall near the Houses of Parliament in London, became (and remains) the focus for annual Remembrance Day celebrations in Britain. The word cenotaph literally means an empty tomb for one who is buried elsewhere. This poem expresses both the public and the private responses to national mourning.

The Cenotaph
September 1919

Not yet will those measureless fields be green again
Where only yesterday the wild sweet blood of wonderful youth
    was shed;
There is a grave whose earth must hold too long, too deep a stain,
Though for ever over it we may speak as proudly as we may tread.
But here, where the watchers by lonely hearths from the thrust of an
    inward sword have more slowly bled,
We shall build the Cenotaph: Victory, winged, with Peace, winged
    too, at the column's head.
And over the stairway, at the foot – oh! here, leave desolate,
    passionate hands to spread
Violets, roses, and laurel, with the small, sweet, twinkling country
    things

Speaking so wistfully of other Springs,
From the little gardens of little places where son or sweetheart was
    born and bred.
In splendid sleep, with a thousand brothers
        To lovers – to mothers
        Here, too, lies he:
Under the purple, the green, the red,
It is all young life: it must break some women's hearts to see
Such a brave, gay coverlet to such a bed!
Only, when all is done and said,
God is not mocked and neither are the dead.
For this will stand in our Market-place –
        Who'll sell, who'll buy
        (Will you or I
Lie each to each with the better grace)?
While looking into every busy whore's and huckster's face
As they drive their bargains, is the Face
Of God: and some young, piteous, murdered face.

Irene Rathbone (1892–1980)

From *We That Were Young* (1932)

This novel gives one of the fullest accounts of the lives of women during the war. The following passage comes from the end of the novel, and shows how Rathbone gives an historical perspective to women's ambivalent attitude to the war. Joan, the central character, tries to explain her feelings about the war to a woman ten years' younger.

'Joan, can I come in? Your aunt said I should probably find you up here. I just …'

A young smooth face, rose-tinted and radiant, was in the doorway. Joan stared at it.

'Molly,' she cried out, 'don't let your young men go to the war! Don't let any of them go to the war! Nothing's worth it!'

'Go to the war, Joan? Are you dotty?'

Joan looked dazed, then blinked, and slightly turned her head.

'No – no, of course – it's different.'

'Joan – *dear*!' Molly laughed, and with an impulsive movement dropped on the hearth-rug. Then seeing papers lying about, said: 'Oh Armistice Day? Is that it? Is that what …?'

'No,' said Joan, 'that's the merest chance. The *day* means nothing. It was just that I saw … My goodness,' she exclaimed softly, her eyes on Molly's upturned face, 'you are *young*!'

Molly caught the something special in the atmosphere, and became all Joan's – though she had come in full of herself.

'Not so very,' she smiled. 'Twenty-five.'

'Extraordinary ... Can you believe,' Joan continued, with queer passion in her voice, 'that *we* were all young once? You can't, of course. But we were! Betty and me, and all our generation – all our brothers and our friends. No other generation ever was so young or ever will be. We were the youth of the world, we were on the crest of life, and we were the war. No one above us counted, and no one below. Youth and the war were the same thing – youth and the war were us.' Her voice dropped. 'But why us, specially? That's the unanswerable question. Why just us? The knife cut so close – above and below.'

'How you must have cursed the war,' murmured Molly.

'We did – we did. But looking back, now, I think we loved it too. Oh, it's so difficult to explain.' Joan had risen, and had wandered over to the window, where she stood looking out, unseeingly. 'So difficult not to put one's present emotions back into that period. At the time, you see, the war was so ordinary – it was just our life. Yes, we hated it, and loved it, both. Loved it only because we gave so much to it, and because it was bound up with our youngness – rather like an unhappy school. It was *our* war, you see. And although it was so every-dayish at the time, and we were so sickened with it, it seems, now, to have a sort of ghastly glamour.' She paused. 'Our hearts are there – unwillingly – for always. It was our war.'

Herbert Read (1893–1968)

One of the most influential literary and art critics of his day, Herbert Read served in France throughout the Great War. This poem 'To a Conscript of 1940' (1944) expresses the feelings of disillusionment shared by many of the soldiers who survived the First World War and lived to see the Second.

To a Conscript of 1940

Qui n'a pas une fois désespéré de l'honneur, ne sera jamais un héros.

GEORGES BERNANOS

A soldier passed me in the freshly fallen snow
His footsteps muffled, his face unearthly grey;
And my heart gave a sudden leap
As I gazed on a ghost of five-and-twenty years ago.

I shouted Halt! and my voice had the old accustomed ring
And he obeyed it as it was obeyed
In the shrouded days when I too was one
Of an army of young men marching

Into the unknown. He turned towards me and I said:
'I am one of those who went before you
Five-and-twenty years ago: one of the many who never returned,
Of the many who returned and yet were dead.

We went where you are going, into the rain and the mud;
We fought as you will fight
With death and darkness and despair;
We gave what you will give – our brains and our blood.

We think we gave in vain. The world was not renewed.
There was hope in the homestead and anger in the streets
But the old world was restored and we returned
To the dreary field and workshop, and the immemorial feud

Of rich and poor. Our victory was our defeat.
Power was retained where power had been misused
And youth was left to sweep away
The ashes that the fires had strewn beneath our feet.
But one thing we learned: there is no glory in the deed
Until the soldier wears a badge of tarnished braid;
There are heroes who have heard the rally and have seen
The glitter of a garland round their head.

Theirs is the hollow victory. They are deceived.
But you, my brother and my ghost, if you can go
Knowing that there is no reward, no certain use
In all your sacrifice, then honour is reprieved.

To fight without hope is to fight with grace,
The self reconstructed, the false heart repaired.'
Then I turned with a smile, and he answered my salute
As he stood against the fretted hedge, which was like white lace.

Isaac Rosenberg (1890–1918)

'Returning, We Hear the Larks' (1917) and letters from *The Complete Works of Isaac Rosenbery* (1937)

'Returning, We Hear the Larks' is one of Rosenberg's best-known poems. In its title and theme it provides part of the inspiration for Sebastian Faulks' novel *Birdsong*.

Rosenberg's letters are revealing because they express not only the feelings of a poet but of an ordinary private soldier towards the life he is being forced to live. The extracts from the letters are printed here with their original spelling and punctuation.

Returning, We Hear the Larks
Sombre the night is.
And though we have our lives, we know
What sinister threat lurks there.

Dragging these anguished limbs, we only know
This poison-blasted track opens on our camp –
On a little safe sleep.

But hark! joy – joy – strange joy.
Lo! heights of night ringing with unseen larks.
Music showering on our upturned list'ning faces.

Death could drop from the dark
As easily as song –
But song only dropped,
Like a blind man's dream on the sand
By dangerous tides,
Like a girl's dark hair for she dreams no ruin lies there,
Or her kisses where a serpent hides.

To Lascelles Abercrombie [March 11, 1916]

DEAR SIR

Your letter was sent to me from home and it gave me a lot of pleasure. I really wonder whether my things are worth the trouble you have taken in analysing them, but if you think they are, and from your letter, you do, of course I should feel encouraged. I send you here my two latest poems, which I have managed to write, though in the utmost distress of mind, or perhaps because of it. Believe me the army is the most detestable invention on this earth and nobody but a private in the army knows what it is to be a slave

I wonder whether your muse has been sniffing gunpowder.

Thank you for your good wishes.

        Yours sincerely

        ISAAC ROSENBERG

To Mrs Cohen

DEAR MRS COHEN

We are on a long march and Im writing this on the chance of getting it off; so you should know I received your papers and also your letter. The notice in the Times of your book is true – especially about your handling of metre. It is an interesting number. The Poetry Review you sent is good – the articles are too breathless, and want more packing, I think. The poems by the soldier are vigourous but, I feel a bit commonplace. I did not like Rupert Brookes begloried sonnets for the same reason. What I mean is second hand phrases 'lambent fires etc takes from its reality and strength. It should be approached in a colder way, more abstract, with less of the million feelings everybody feels; or all these should be concentrated in one distinguished emotion. Walt Whitman in 'Beat, drums, beat, has said the noblest thing on war ...

        Yours sincerely

        ISAAC ROSENBERG

Siegfried Sassoon (1886–1967)

'On Passing the New Menin Gate', 'To One Who Was With Me in the War' (1928)
and from *Siegfried's Journey* (1945)

The two poems offer contrasting meditations on the war seen in retrospect.

The autobiographical account of the moment when he completed the writing of
his Protest Statement (see pages 30–31), shows Sassoon only too well aware of the
different ways in which his actions may be interpreted.

On Passing the New Menin Gate

Who will remember, passing through this Gate,
The unheroic Dead who fed the guns?
Who shall absolve the foulness of their fate, –
Those doomed, conscripted, unvictorious ones?
    Crudely renewed, the Salient holds its own.
    Paid are its dim defenders by this pomp;
    Paid, with a pile of peace-complacent stone,
    The armies who endured that sullen swamp.

Here was the world's worst wound. And here with pride
'Their name liveth for ever,' the Gateway claims.
Was ever an immolation so belied
As these intolerably nameless names?
Well might the Dead who struggled in the slime
Rise and deride this sepulchre of crime.

To One Who Was With Me in the War

It was too long ago – that Company which we served with …
We call it back in visual fragments, you and I,
Who seem, ourselves, like relics casually preserved with
Our mindfulness of old bombardments when the sky
With blundering din blinked cavernous.
                     Yet a sense of power
Invades us when, recapturing an ungodly hour
Of ante-zero crisis, in one thought we've met
To stand in some redoubt of Time, – to share again
All but the actual wetness of the flare-lit rain,
All but the living presences who haunt us yet
With gloom-patrolling eyes.
                Remembering, we forget

Much that was monstrous, much that clogged our souls with clay
When hours were guides who led us by the longest way –
And when the worst had been endured could still disclose
Another worst to thwart us ...
                              We forget our fear ...
And, while the uncouth Event begin to lour less near,
Discern the mad magnificence whose storm-light throws
Wild shadows on these after-thoughts that send your brain
Back beyond Peace, exploring sunken ruinous roads.

It thus happened that, about midnight on the day my portrait was finished, I sat alone in the club library with a fair copy of the 'statement' before me on the writing-table. The words were now solidified and unalterable. My brain was unable to scrutinise their meaning any more. They had become merely a sequence of declamatory sentences, designed to let me in for what appeared to be a moral equivalent of 'going over the top'; and, at the moment, the Hindenberg Line seemed preferable in retrospect. For the first time, I allowed myself to reflect upon the consequences of my action and to question my strength to endure them. Possibly what I disliked most was the prospect of being misunderstood and disapproved of by my fellow officers. Some of them would regard my behaviour as a disgrace to the Regiment. Others would assume that I had gone a bit crazy. How many of them, I wondered, would give me credit for having done it for the sake of the troops who were at the Front? I had never heard any of them use the word pacifist except in a contemptuous and intolerant way, and in my dispirited mood I felt that my protest would have a pretty poor reception among them. Going to a window, I looked out at the searchlights probing the dark sky. Down below, the drone of London rumbled on. The streets were full of soldiers getting what enjoyment they could out of their leave. And there, on that sheet of paper under the green-shaded lamp, were the words I had just transcribed.

'I believe that this war, upon which I entered as a war of defence and liberation, has now become a war of aggression and conquest.'

To the soldiers it didn't matter, one way or the other. They all wanted it to stop, but most of them would say that the Boches had got to be beaten somehow, and the best thing to hope for was 'getting back to Blighty with a cushy wound'.

Jon Stallworthy

From *Wilfred Owen* (1974)

This is still one of the most widely admired biographies written about any of the major literary figures from the Great War. This passage describes Owen's death on 4 November 1918 during the crossing of the Sambre–Oise Canal.

Seeing there was no hope for the survivors or their bridge without more effective covering fire, a nineteen-year-old 2nd Lieutenant of the Manchesters, James Kirk, snatched up a Lewis gun and four magazines and ran down to the water's edge. He climbed on to a raft, paddled to within ten yards of the German machine-gunners and opened fire, forcing them to take cover behind their parapet. Those few precious minutes enabled the Engineers, Major Waters and Sapper Archibald, to finish mending the bridge. Then Kirk's machine-gun stopped firing. The last of his magazines was empty. He was wounded in the arm and in the face, but more magazines were paddled out to him, and again he opened fire from his tilting raft. Behind him the bridge was pushed out and two platoons scrambled across. Almost at once, as a lucky shell severed the pontoons, they were cut off and James Kirk fell forward over his gun, shot through the head.

To the right of the 2nd Manchesters, the 16th Lancashire Fusiliers were in the same perilous predicament. Commanding them that day was Acting Lieutenant-Colonel Marshall of the ten wounds who, not to be outdone by his former Battalion, called for a party of volunteers to repair the broken bridge in front of his position. They rose to him and wrestled with the wire and the small cork rafts at the water's edge until all were killed or wounded. Standing over them, fully exposed on the bank, Marshall for a moment turned his broad back on the enemy and bellowed for another party of volunteers. Again they came forward and he cursed and encouraged them as they went to work. Miraculously, enough survived to repair the bridge and push it out over the whipped water. Marshall led his men across, only to fall on the far bank with his eleventh and final wound.

Through this hurricane the small figure of Wilfred Owen walked backwards and forwards between his men, patting them on the shoulder, saying 'Well done' and 'You're doing very well, my boy'. He was at the water's edge, giving a hand with some duckboards, when he was hit and killed.

By midday the remnants of the 2nd Manchesters were on the other side of the Canal, having crossed south of Ors by means of a floating bridge supported on kerosene tins. And seven days later, as the guns fell silent on the Western Front, the survivors piled their rifles, took off their helmets, and went to sleep; the living like the dead.

Rebecca West (1892–1983)

From *The Return of the Soldier* (1918)

One of the earliest novels which explores the anxiety with which women waited for the return of their men from the war. In this novel, West dramatises the acuteness of this anxiety by having the shell-shocked soldier return unable to remember the woman to whom he is married.

That day its beauty was an affront to me, because like most Englishwomen of my time I was wishing for the return of a soldier. Disregarding the national interest and everything except the keen prehensile gesture of our hearts towards him, I wanted to snatch my cousin Christopher from the wars and seal him in this green pleasantness his wife and I now looked upon. Of late I had had bad dreams about him. By night I saw Chris running across the brown rottenness of No Man's Land, starting back here because he trod upon a hand, not even looking there because of the awfulness of an unburied head, and not till my dream was packed full of horror did I see him pitch forward on his knees as he reached safety – if it was that. For on the war-films I have seen men slip down as softly from the trench parapet, and none but the grimmer philosophers would say that they had reached safety by their fall. And when I escaped into wakefulness it was only to lie stiff and think of stories I had heard in the boyish voice, that rings indomitable yet has most of its gay notes flattened, of the modern subaltern.

"We were all of us in a barn one night, and a shell came along. My pal sang out, *'Help me, old man, I've got no legs!'* and I had to answer, *'I can't, old man, I've got no hands!'*"

Well, such are the dreams of Englishwomen to-day; I could not complain. But I wished for the return of our soldier.

4 | Critical approaches

- How does the Great War fit into the cultural and literary history of the 20th century?

- How important are issues such as gender and national identity in discussing Great War texts?

Part 4 of *The Great War in British Literature* looks both at the literary response of critics to the writing that emerged directly out of the fighting of 1914–18 and reviews the ways in which recent critical debate about the Great War has shifted. This debate seeks to ask how the Great War fits into, and itself helps to shape, the cultural history of Britain in the 20th century. In this debate questions of language, gender, class, nationalism and politics are raised alongside (or sometimes instead of) questions about the literary significance and value of individual texts and writers. The different ways in which texts dealing with the Great War may be read become as important, for some critics, as the texts themselves. This in turn leads back to questions about the boundaries of Great War literature as a genre: which texts, and which writers, can be included and which should be excluded from the canon – and on what grounds?

Anthologising the Great War

A good example of the problems these questions raise can be seen in the anthologies of First World War poetry. During and just after 1914–18, anthologies tended to promote a patriotic and heroic definition of war poetry: they had titles such as *Valour and Vision* and *The Muse in Arms*. As has already been seen, the poems by writers such as Owen and Sassoon appeared first in literary magazines and did not find their way into these anthologies. In 1942, *An Anthology of War Poetry*, edited by Julian Symonds, was published by Penguin Books – one of the very first paperback anthologies of war poetry. Over twenty years elapsed before the next generation of anthologies appeared: *Up The Line To Death* (1964), edited by Brian Gardner, and *Men Who March Away* (1965) by Ian Parsons. These books concentrated mainly on poets who had actually fought in the war, and exclusively on poetry written by men. *The Penguin Book of First World War Poetry*, edited by Jon Silkin, appeared in 1979 and contained poems by three women writers; by the time that anthology had reached its third edition, the editor had increased the number of women to eight. In a special Note to the 1996 edition Silkin wrote:

> … the inclusion of these additional poems registers, not elegy, but the pain and grief of those who do not kill, do not get slaughtered,

but whose role seems to be restricted (literally) to enduring deprivation – for instance, the unredeemed loss of those who are loved. I needed to find poems the responses of which were neither diluted or amerced ['punished' – an interestingly revealing choice of word on Silkin's part] by patriotism – which I still believe to be a manufactured and immoral composite – and which fulfilled the requirement of literary excellence ... I would not have included these poems had I not been convinced. To be so, I had to expand my emotional register to include the tenderness as well as the outrage of grief. And I had to apprehend the living response to a life without the one who is loved, and who has been destroyed not by death but by war.

Silkin wrote this Note as a reply to the question, were the extra poems by women poets added to the 1996 edition 'included under feminist pressure'? and he admitted, 'I feel I must say that feminism did require me to consider, again, as scrupulously as I could, why, with the following exceptions, all the poets in the anthology are male.'

Silkin was one of the most thoughtful of English critics and editors of the literature of the Great War (see also Further reading, Part 6, pages 121–123). The fact that as late as 1996 he was admitting the need to rethink what was and was not admissible as war poetry makes clear how the canon of Great War writing is not (and perhaps cannot be) finally agreed. It also makes clear how a movement (feminism) which is not in essence a literary movement at all can change the way people think about a subject such as the Great War in literary terms.

One of the most significant books published in between the first and third editions of Silkin's anthology was the anthology *Scars Upon My Heart* (1981) whose editor, Catherine Reilly, had discovered that there were 'no fewer than 2225 British individuals, men and women, servicemen and civilians, who had written verse on the theme of this most terrible war. Of these 2225 at least 532 were women ...'. Catherine Reilly was quite explicit that 'the present collection is the result of curiosity as to why the work of most of the 532 women poets traced in my bibliographical study should have apparently faded into oblivion' and she added, 'The introduction of Women's Studies into the academic curriculum of many universities and colleges makes it imperative that all feminine viewpoints should be explored.' The impact of her anthology has been to enlarge the way in which war poetry is defined, and hence to make other editors such as Jon Silkin revise their own criteria for selecting writers for their books. This in turn has affected the way in which readers read about the Great War: the perspective has been altered, and cannot be narrowed again. What Silkin described as the 'tenderness as well as the outrage of grief' has to be part of any critical response to the literature of the subject.

▶ Silkin wrote of 'literary excellence' as one of the criteria for including a poem in his anthology; Reilly was anxious to be inclusive in *Scars Upon My Heart* and described it as 'an anthology of poetry and verse', implying that not all the pieces chosen met the test of 'literary excellence'. How important do you think 'literary excellence' would be as a basis for selecting writing about the Great War to go into an anthology you were editing?

The war poets as critics

Those writers who survived the war not only spent the next decade writing about their experiences; they also wrote about, edited and introduced the work of those who had not survived. Thus Edmund Blunden edited the poetry of Wilfred Owen and, later, of Ivor Gurney; Sassoon wrote a Foreword to the *Complete Works of Isaac Rosenberg*. In describing Rosenberg's achievement in poetry, Sassoon was keen to emphasise his qualities as a writer rather than his status as a war poet:

> In reading and re-reading these poems I have been strongly impressed by their depth and integrity. I have found a sensitive and vigorous mind energetically interested in experimenting with language ... His experiments were a strenuous effort for impassioned expression; his imagination had a sinewy and muscular aliveness; often he saw things in terms of sculpture, but he did not carve or chisel; he *modelled* words with fierce energy and aspiration, finding ecstasy in form ... Watching him working with words, I find him a poet of movement; words which express movement are often used by him and are essential to his natural utterance.

▶ Read 'Returning, We Hear the Larks' (page 90) and 'Dead Man's Dump' and then try to apply Sassoon's comments about Rosenberg's handling of language to these poems. In particular, do you agree with Sassoon about the importance, for Rosenberg, of words which express movement? Does it affect the way you read these poems if you ignore the fact that they were written by someone who was labelled (after his death) as a 'war poet'?

Sassoon particularly admired Rosenberg's poem 'Break of Day in the Trenches' of which he wrote:

> Sensuous front-line existence is there, hateful and repellent, unforgettable and inescapable. And beyond this poem I see the poems that he might have written after the war, and the life he might have lived when life began again beyond and behind those trenches

which were the limbo of all sane humanity and world-improving imagination. For the spirit of poetry looks beyond life's trench-lines. And Isaac Rosenberg was naturally empowered with something of the divine spirit which touches our human clay to sublimity of expression.

These comments are as revealing about Sassoon as they are about Rosenberg. To describe, nearly twenty years after the end of the Great War, the trenches as 'the limbo of all sane humanity and world-improving imagination' is to condemn the war as a form of madness and as an interruption to the real job of the artist: to use his or her imagination to improve the world. (Compare this with the discussion between the soldiers in John Drinkwater's 1917 play $x = o$ (see Part 3, page 79). Sassoon's view of art and of the artist is a definitely Romantic one: he claims that the artist receives a form of divine inspiration 'which touches our human clay to sublimity of expression'. Statements such as these Wordsworth and Coleridge might have approved of; but modernism (or the 20th century generally) would not have found them easy to accept.

Edmund Blunden, too, revealed much about his own attitudes to war poetry and to the Great War. Writing a Foreword to Brian Gardner's anthology *Up the Line To Death* (1964) he noted:

> It is a singular thing for one who passed through the valley of the shadow so long ago to be returning to it, fifty years afterwards, and yet it is a great moment when these survivors discover good companions in the new generation ... Of this new generation Brian Gardner is a representative. He has the world as in his time, but he longs to do homage to those who looked beyond death, or who were horrified by schematic death into a new poetry, half a century since. His anthology of the Brooke, Sassoon, Owen generation, though one or two earlier books of the sort are not yet dead asleep on our shelves, is not only a literary achievement of the first order, but a testimony of the spirit of man worthy of the 'lost generation'.

Blunden's comments here (admittedly taken from a Foreword designed to promote the anthology rather than from a formal critical essay) are significant first for emphasising the concept of companionship as an enduring legacy of the war. For many soldiers, the experience of close companionship in the trenches had compensated for (and sometimes even outweighed) the actual horrors of the War; for the survivors, it had in fact made the experience one of the most important and even rewarding in their lives. Second, Blunden believed that the mechanical and mechanised horror of the war ('schematic death') had created a new poetry:

though not himself a modernist, he understood how the conditions of the war had made the old ways and the old themes of writing obsolete. Third, it is interesting that Blunden was willing to group Brooke, Sassoon and Owen together as members of the same generation, rather than to distance Sassoon and Owen from Brooke as most critics before and since have done. (See also Part 1, page 15.)

Critical attitudes 1920–60

It has already been suggested (see Part 1, pages 37–39) that the 1920s and 1930s were not sympathetic to the war poets. Perhaps the most celebrated example of this lack of sympathy was to be found in *The Oxford Book of Modern Verse* (1936) edited by W.B. Yeats. This influential anthology contained no poetry by Wilfred Owen, and Yeats justified his decision to omit him by claiming that 'passive suffering is not a theme for poetry'; however, a more telling argument was that the surviving poets Sassoon and Blunden were too closely identified with the now outdated *Georgian Poetry* anthologies, and Richard Aldington had, by the 1930s, largely abandoned poetry for fiction. Blunden's cry in the poem 'To W.O. and his Kind'

> Would you were not dust [I wish you were not dead]

is both a lament for a lost companion (although the two men never actually met while Owen was alive) and a reproach to the younger generation who have forgotten what Owen had had to say about war. However, the note that is often heard among critics writing in the 1930s and 1940s about the war poets of 1914–18 is one of impatience with writers who had not been able leave the experiences of the Great War behind. To Edmund Blunden's statement 'I must go over the ground again' came back the question 'Why?' The following comments on Sassoon come from an essay, 'War and the Writer' published by a widely-read literary historian, Ifor Evans, in 1948:

> Sassoon's limitation, when viewed from the perspective of these later years, is that his imagination has remained fixed in the experiences of the war years of 1914–18. Nothing has happened later that could be admitted into the intimate places of his mind, and indeed so absolute was the fixation that later events were not permitted to intrude even if they could have helped to interpret the war crisis which he was attempting to elucidate. This is particularly notable in the autobiography [*Siegfried's Journey*, 1945] where sometimes he seems to write as if nothing of importance had happened since 1918.
> (*English Literature Between the Wars*)

Evans was no more tolerant and no less confident in his comments on the fiction of the Great War. After dismissing *All Quiet on the Western Front* (by the German novelist Erich Maria Remarque) as 'a crude and sentimental volume with a strain that is almost hysterical', he applauded British and American novels published in the same year, 1929: Richard Aldington's *Death of a Hero* and Ernest Hemingway's *A Farewell to Arms* were, he said, 'far more genuinely realistic and authentic than Remarque'. However, the conclusion Evans went on to reach about the literature of the Great War was an important one, if only because it put an end to discussion of the writers for another fifteen years, and because it blamed poets and novelists for the British political attitudes of the 1930s – in particular for appeasement, the idea that the best way to deal with Hitler was not to confront him but to allow him as much of his own way as possible:

> If one has to summarise the effect of literature on modern life in England, it may be advanced that despite all its sincerity the ultimate result of this 'horror' literature of the war of 1914–18 was an unhappy one. It bred in its readers a mood of fear, which was negative and ineffective. The soldier was too ready to indulge in a mixture of sentiment and hysteria in order to revenge himself on the civilian whom he regarded as sheltered from his dangers. The war literature of the years 1929 and 1930 prepared for the political passivism of the thirties and its refusal in many minds to see that Europe was preparing for a new barbarism. Yet the writers themselves must not be condemned. They were expressing the shock which civilised man felt when he first met modern warfare, particularly in its most dull and degrading form of trench warfare.

Critical attitudes after the 1960s

From the 1960s onwards, the response to the literature of the Great War became more analytical, and the scope more comprehensive. Bernard Bergonzi's *Heroes Twilight: A Study of the Literature of the Great War* (1965) and Jon Silkin's *Out of Battle: The Poetry of the Great War* (1972) helped to establish a critical framework within which the texts of and about the period – although still almost exclusively by male writers – could be discussed.

In his long Introduction to *The Penguin Book of First World War Poetry*, Silkin defines four 'stages of consciousness' which can be found in war poetry (and prose). The first, which he says is exhibited in Rupert Brooke's sonnets, is 'not so much a stage in consciousness as a passive reflection of, or conduit for, the prevailing patriot ideas, and the cant that's contingent on most social abstract impulsions'. The second (embodied for Silkin in the poetry of Siegfried Sassoon) is an outright protest against what Sassoon called 'the political errors and insincerities for which the fighting men are being sacrificed'. Silkin suggests that 'it is the "callous complacency" of the civilian' which is the target of this attack. The third stage Silkin sees as 'compassion – strength of feeling' which is not to be confused with the 'the more intimate response of pity and tenderness', and this stage he identifies in the writing of Wilfred Owen, though he warns, 'The danger with Owen's compassion is that it can tend to self-indulgence, and perhaps even attempt to assuage the guilt of the killer.' It is Isaac Rosenberg who, for Silkin, embodies the fourth and highest stage of consciousness 'where the anger and compassion are merged, with extreme intelligence, into an active desire for change, a change that will re-align the elements of human society in such a way as to make it more creative and fruitful'.

▶ Silkin quotes from Rosenberg's poem 'Dead Man's Dump' to illustrate the qualities that he considers place Rosenberg above Owen as the finest poet of the Great War. Read the poem yourself and decide whether you can understand how it represents Silkin's fourth stage of consciousness.

▶ Silkin adds, 'the complexity of Rosenberg's concerns is matched with a richness of imagery and rhythm – movement overall – which is sensuously more alert, I think, than Owen's. Ever so slightly, Owen's language suffers from the settled quality of the "spokesman". For whom, and ... to whom (at that time) was Rosenberg speaking?' Compare any poem by Rosenberg with 'Spring Offensive' by Owen to see whether you agree with Jon Silkin's judgement here. In what way do you think Owen can be described as a 'spokesman'?

Gender and feminist approaches

One of the most obvious but most significant facts about life in the trenches is that it was a life lived by men among men; women, unless serving as nurses, ambulance drivers or relief workers, did not feature near the Front at all. The idea that the war was man's work produced many tensions both within society and in personal relationships. Autobiographies such as *Testament of Youth* by Vera Brittain and novels such as *Bid Me to Live* by H.D. or *We That Were Young* by Irene Rathbone all illustrate these tensions. At the same time, the fact that women were able to take advantage of men's absence to gain employment and a greater degree of personal freedom led to an anxiety expressed very frequently in the poetry of the Great War. Recent critics have taken this as a starting point for an analysis of the writing of the period. Here, for example is a discussion of the 'trench poem' [in other words, poetry written from direct experience of conditions in the trenches] as 'a poetry of passivity':

The First World War represented a great opportunity for women in society, in the work force, and in culture generally ... The absence of men allowed women unprecedented freedom, while it simultaneously deprived combatant men of their former masculine prerogatives, such as job-choice, physical well-being, virility and life. Thus many men came to blame women not only for taking advantage of men's predicament, but for somehow inflicting the damage themselves ... The trench poem is a poetry of passivity. In this it finds its justification: passivity is the ethical high ground. Yet passivity is also untenable: the responsibility of both inflicting and articulating the suffering of his men often becomes more than the officer-poet can bear. The result is active violence against the enemy (both Sassoon and Owen were decorated war heroes) and verbal violence against the non-combatants. Moreover some of the most direct attacks against non-combatants are aimed specifically at women.

(James S. Campbell 'Misogyny, Homosexuality and Passivity in World War 1 Poetry', *ELH*, 1997, Vol 64, part 3)

This approach to the literature of the Great War can be illuminating: noting that both Wilfred Owen and Siegfried Sassoon were homosexual, critics often point to poems such as Sassoon's 'Glory of Women' to illustrate the apparent contempt that some of the war poets showed towards women:

You love us when we're heroes home, on leave,
Or wounded in a mentionable place.
You worship decorations; you believe
That chivalry redeems the war's disgrace.
You make us shells. You listen with delight,
By tales of dirt and danger fondly thrilled ...

These views attributed by Sassoon to women were, of course, a travesty of what many women actually felt. Vera Brittain, who is so often taken as the representative voice of women in the Great War, wrote to her brother after his arrival in the trenches:

I feel very lonely now you have gone; the days seem to drag more and to be longer than ever. I only wish my duty were as obvious as yours; one's duty is certainly the only thing left to do, but it is a little difficult when one is not quite sure what one's duty is.

(*Letters from a Lost Generation*)

Less than two weeks later, after learning the details of how her fiancé Roland Leighton had died, she had decided she could not go back to Oxford but must continue nursing:

> Nations may fall, & religions may fail, and there may be a Hereafter & there may not – but amid all these things, amid death & grief and disaster & danger, the mind of man is unconquerable, if it choose. So I am beginning to feel – vaguely & unwillingly, it is true – that to leave this hospital [she was nursing at a military hospital in London] even though I hate it, would be defeat. I am beginning to think I shall not leave it, except of course for one reason, & that is if I got the chance of War-work of any kind, preferably France. Otherwise, if I don't get any chance, I ought to stick to it, let it cost me what it will. That's one thing that Roland's agony has made me feel. No one He loved must be unworthy of Him …

▶ Look at this way this letter is written. How do you react to the diction (choice of language), imagery and manner of writing (for instance, the capital H for pronouns referring to Roland)?

A specifically feminist criticism of writing from the Great War explores the way writing by women expresses the ambivalent feelings of women towards the war and the ambivalent feelings of men towards women in the war. A book that is well worth comparing with Vera Brittain's letters and with *Testament of Youth* is Irene Rathbone's *We That Were Young* (1932), a novel which centres on the wartime experiences of women working as YMCA volunteers, as V.A.D.s and as munitions workers. Like Vera Brittain herself (whose relationship with her brother Edward was perhaps the closest and most problematic of her life) the heroine of *We That Were Young*, Joan, is closest to her younger brother Jimmy:

> *We That Were Young* may also be more representative of women's ambivalence about the war because, despite its graphic descriptions of wounded men, the reader's outrage is controlled by corresponding passages that glamorise and eroticise the war experience in descriptions of handsome bodies of marching troops, the girls' responses to the knees of Scottish warriors in their kilts, the way the women change into evening dresses to dance in London clubs with uniformed soldiers. This tug between the glamour and horror of war was real, and it also appears in the work of May Sinclair and the letters of Vera Brittain, part of the brother/sister incestuous "we" of the narrative of the generational war, often accompanied by the wish of the New Women, liberated by the suffrage movement and already

trained by that movement to think of themselves as part of a righteous army, to be soldiers themselves and to fight alongside their brothers ... The incest plot lurks beneath the surface of nationalist war writing. English poetry by men in this period is homoerotic. Women writers mourn the loss of their suffragette-soldier selves in the deaths of their brothers. They mourn the loss of sisterhood in political struggle, their own hopes for autonomy and freedom, for that is what they really sacrificed, in mourning the men of their generation.

(Jane Marcus 'Afterword' to *We That Were Young*, 1989)

Jane Marcus's view of the novel extracts a serious sub-text, and offers an insight into ways of reading women's writing about the Great War. The tensions between men and women, masculine and feminine stereotypes, between attitudes to Germany and England, between combatant and non-combatant – all of these can be seen in the novel's use of images which are given a symbolic significance:

The Nurse's Text [Marcus sees the novel as an 'anaesthetised' narrative in which the horrors of the war are dulled by the alleged sentimentalism of the writing] has given the reader-survivors a picture album of their war work. The most vivid for me is of the young woman being scalped by her machine in the munitions factory because she cannot bear binding up her long hair in a cap. Equally memorable is Joan's feverish dream that her infected arm has become a grotesque German sausage. Inflamed by the wounds it has probed and cleared of shrapnel and bullets, the arm, the agent of her healing power as a nurse, becomes the enemy, German, phallic, the nightmare of the guilt male writers also projected upon the disturbing figure of the nurse, who is blamed in men's writing about the war for wounding or emasculating those whom she heals. Her capacity to bear this survivor's guilt, to hallucinate her own arm as the enemy's gun and to repress it, recovering and continuing the work of patching up bodies and culture, is a testament to her generation's incredibly successful ability to bear the burden of cultural representation, to wear the nurse's uniform, to be the blank page, but to write on its starchy surface the record of her work.

▶ Read the following extract from *We That Were Young* and then consider Jane Marcus's analysis (above) of the passage. Do you find her interpretation of the imagery convincing? What do her references to the 'reader-survivor' and to the 'survivor's guilt' suggest about the relationship of a reader today to the subject matter of literature about the Great War?

Her arm throbbed. From the gramophone in one of the officers' wards came the strains of the 'Broken Doll'. Over and over and over again that inane and vacuously sentimental song droned its way up through the windows.

> 'And when you go away,
> You'll be sorry some day,
> You left behind a bro-ken do-oll.'

The next day passed in much the same way, except that during the hot afternoon the 'Broken Doll' was varied now and then by 'The Only Girl in the World'. For this slight relief Joan was thankful, as her head was becoming worse, and her arm, now swollen to the dimensions of a nightmare German sausage, was causing her a lot of pain. She looked at it with stupid eyes as it lay crimson and tight-skinned on the counterpane. She didn't recognise it. She thought at moments that it must be her leg, which had somehow got outside the bedclothes.

Nationhood, myth and history: the Great War in British literature today

The Great War has now become as much a part of the mythology as of the history of the 20th century, and writers and critics have been keen to explore the ways in which this mythology has been created. The relationship between the war and ideas of what is meant by England ('This England', 'some corner of a foreign field that is forever England', etc.) has become an important question for anyone revisiting the literature of the Great War to understand the importance of this literature in its cultural context. At one point in *We That Were Young* Irene Rathbone writes:

> What was the use of winning the war, Joan cried to herself in sudden despair, if none of the men who won it were to live? The papers were forever quoting 'Who dies if England lives? But after all what *was* England? The old men who sat at home, and in clubs, and gloatingly discussed the war? The bustling business men who thought they ran it? The women with aching hearts? Or the young manhood of the nation – that part of the nation that should be working, mating, begetting, but which now was being cut down? There was no question – the last. And in a year or two there'd be no 'England'.

Those are the thoughts put into the mouth of a fictional woman by someone who had herself lived through the war. For her, only one of the four groups of people she lists – the 'young manhood of the nation' (note the difference between the rhetorical flourish of this phrase and 'the old men who sat at home' and 'the bustling business men') – represent England: significantly, she excludes herself (one of the 'women with aching hearts') from being able to represent England.

The vision of England before the Great War as some kind of paradise is, of course, part of the myth. Philip Larkin's poem 'MCMXIV' is both an evocation of the England of 1914 and a criticism of it: the idea of a golden country –

> the place names all hazed over
> With flowering grasses, and fields
> Shadowing Domesday lines –

– that stretches back to an immemorial past is a necessary part of the myth because what followed, the unimaginable reality of the Western Front, replaced one myth with another. Both landscapes (pre-war and wartime) exist today in memory and in imagination, not in reality. One of the most penetrating of Larkin's critics, Andrew Swarbrick, has commented that the poem

> ... is not a simple piece of patriotic nostalgia. It knows that it is dealing with cultural myths as potent as those purveyed in the advertising images of other poems [for example, 'Sunny Prestatyn']. The lines of men queuing up to enlist, 'Grinning as if it were all / An August Bank Holiday lark', are viewed with pathos but also a subdued irony which surfaces again at the end of the poem: 'the men / Leaving the gardens tidy, / The thousands of marriages / Lasting a little while longer' ... So the end of the poem, 'Never such innocence, / Never before or since ... Never such innocence again', with its liturgical rhythms asserts ... an emotional attitude rather than accepted fact. It is self-consciously rhetorical and knows it is dealing in myths.
> (Andrew Swarbrick *Out of Reach: The Poetry of Philip Larkin*, 1995)

This sense of dealing in myths becomes very important, finally, when assessing the most recent novels about the Great War, Sebastian Faulks' *Birdsong* and Pat Barker's *Regeneration* trilogy. *Birdsong* puts the imaginative reconstructions of the Somme offered by the author himself side by side with the incoherent memories of the now ancient survivors; in so doing the reader has to ask which version of history (reality/memory or imaginative/fictitious) is more 'true'. Pat Barker's novels are concerned with the ways in which the minds of men cope with seeing what they should not have seen. Both books recreate the Europe of 1914; both adopt what the critic Bernard Bergonzi (author of *Heroes Twilight*, 1965, one of the most important critical surveys of British writing in the Great War) calls 'an essentially mythic' approach:

Such works may draw in detail on historical scholarship, but their perception of the war, being mythic, is fixed, static and a-historical. It is nevertheless deeply rooted in the national consciousness, nourished by the theatrical popularity of *Oh What a Lovely War!* and the generation of school students who study the war poets in English Literature lessons ... Barker's mythic bias is why she is not very interested in getting her history right; she is more concerned in establishing a connection between the myth and certain preoccupations of the present time: gender roles, feminism, psychotherapy, false memory syndrome, the sexual abuse of children. Perhaps she believes, in the fashion of high modernist mythopoeia [the making of myths], that all wars, whether the First World War, the Second or the Vietnam War, are ultimately the same war.

(Bernard Bergonzi 'The *Regeneration* Trilogy' in *Gravesiana*, vol 1.ii, December 1996)

This suggestion that writers such as Pat Barker see all wars, including the Great War, as part of the same war is an appropriate point on which to leave this introduction to critical responses to the Great War in British literature. But, if Bergonzi is right, then attitudes to the Great War in the 20th century have come full circle, for it is important to remember that many of those who went to fight in 1914 saw themselves as embarking on a new Trojan War, or a new Crusade or a new adventure in chivalry. Indeed, for a poet like Edward Thomas, writing in 1915, the British soldier mown down by machine gun fire in France was already resurrected as the English yeoman of history and myth – always willing to defend and die for his country, whatever the war:

The man you saw, – Lob-lie-by-the-fire, Jack Cade,
Jack Smith, Jack Moon, poor Jack of every trade,
Young Jack, or old Jack, or Jack What-d'ye-call,
Jack-in-the-hedge, or Robin-run-by-the-wall,
Robin Hood, Ragged Robin, lazy Bob,
One of the lords of No Man's Land, good Lob, –
Although he was seen dying at Waterloo,
Hastings, Agincourt, and Sedgemoor too, –
Lives yet.

('Lob')

Assignments

1 Contrast the presentation of women during the Great War in any two novels you have read.

2 Look again at the 'four stages of consciousness' applied by Jon Silkin (pages 101–102) to characterise the writing of Rupert Brooke, Siegfried Sassoon, Wilfred Owen and Isaac Rosenberg. Do you agree with the taxonomy (classification, ranking in order of importance) that Silkin proposes, and do you think it can be applied to any writing about the Great War?

3 How helpful and important do you find it to distinguish between 'the literature of the Great War', 'literature from the Great War' and the Great War as a theme in British Literature?

4 Explore some of the ways in which class and gender (key issues of the period of the Great War) are presented in the writing you have studied.

5 | How to write about the Great War in British literature

- What is the relationship between the writer and the reader?

- How far will your own views be influenced by other readers' interpretations?

The writer and the reader

An obvious point first: if you are writing about a particular text it is important to decide what type of text it is, who wrote it and for whom. You also need to ask who reads it today and from what point of view. These questions might seem self-evident, or they might seem baffling; in relation to writing about the Great War, they are basic.

Consider this piece of writing:

> Madame's little inn stands on a hillside and the door commands a view of one of the finest provinces of France. In spring-time a sea of apple-blossom stretches away in all directions. To-day a sea of grey tents stretches away to the left of madame's windows, while to the right khaki figures gather at their favourite rendezvous, the railway bridge.
>
> It is the presence of the railway that has brought madame such wide fame. On the boards of that village station are painted names that will wring the heart of France for ever, and the trains that pass through that countryside daily carry khaki thousands who have sworn to avenge those significant names.

How do you react to this piece of writing? It appeared in an English newspaper in 1918 under the headline 'Madame of the Inn'. The writer signed herself Hilda M. Love, although this may have been a pseudonym. In what ways are the images and descriptions seeking to control the reader's response? How might a reader of 1918 have responded to it? Would the reaction have been different if the passage had been published in 1914 or 1915?

These questions are a reminder of the importance of 'placing' a text when you first encounter it; its reception over time – the way different people in different circumstances on different occasions might respond to it – is a central issue when discussing any text from or about the Great War.

The writer of this piece goes on to describe how soldiers on their way to the Front stop for a couple of hours at this station and are able to enjoy a meal in madame's dining room:

> Her tables are covered with much good fare: the scent of coffee is sniffed as the rarest perfume; there are jugs of hot, foaming milk, slabs of delicious, fresh butter, excellent soup, chickens browned to a turn, omelettes that are something to remember for a lifetime, chipped potatoes and salads that are as crisp as madame's directions to her satellites, cheeses of all kinds besides the famous apple jelly and the good vin ordinaire.
>
> No wonder many a man says as he boards the train, "What's the name of this place? Best feed I've had in France."
>
> I have seen madame at the door of her inn bidding the last of her visitors "Good night" as they departed for the train, her hands on her ample hips, quietly looking after the khaki figures going into the darkness. Down on the line there is noise and bustle, which settles into a great stillness when the train has slowly steamed out into the night.

More questions arise as you begin to focus on this part of the text:

- How can the writer apparently ignore the fact that the 'khaki figures' are going straight back to the fighting? (The only reference to fighting is veiled under the earlier reference to their having 'sworn to avenge those significant names' – in other words, the battlefields such as Ypres, Cambrai and the Somme.)

- Is the irony of describing the soldiers 'going into the darkness' something which a modern reader 'reads back' into the text?

- Has the writer really heard 'many a man' saying what she claims to have heard them say as they board the train? Or is this poetic licence?

- If so, is this an example of (mis)appropriation of experience? Is the writer taking a situation that is full of pathos (men who are about to go back to the Front having a last decent meal before reaching the trenches – 'the condemned man ate a hearty breakfast') and distorting it to provide a cheerful story for civilian readers in Britain?

Authenticity: comparing texts

However, the authenticity of this writing (in a literary, not just a documentary, sense) can be tested by comparing it with this extract from Edmund Blunden's *Undertones of War* (written in 1924 and published in 1928):

The battalion detrains at an unknown siding and its forerunners guide it into unknown M Camp ... Suddenly turning aside we find the Quartermaster and Transport Officer, Swain and Maycock, who, stamping their feet, rejoice with me, and Maycock seizes my shoulders with gloved hand and pretends to dance. These invincible officers have a pleasant surprise for us and, although it is midnight, there is soon a sound of revelry. In a large wooden tavern a cheerful Belgian girl, under the argus-eyed direction of a masculine mother, is soon running hither and thither among the veterans, from colonel to subaltern, with some of the best victuals ever known. Rave on, you savage east, and gloom, you small hours; we will take our ease in our inn, by the red-hot stoves. We have come through.

▶ In what ways does this passage differ from 'Madame of the Inn'? Can the writing of one be described as more 'authentic' or more 'effective' than the other? How does the romanticism of the remembered account given by Blunden differ from that offered by Hilda M. Love?

Blunden spent longer in the front lines than almost any other of the war poets or writers. His whole life afterwards was dominated by his experiences there; during the 1930s he campaigned so hard against the accelerating slide towards the Second World War that he was accused of appeasement and even of sympathising with the Nazis. He saw himself (as many veterans of this and subsequent wars have done) as resembling the Ancient Mariner who could get no rest from the nightmares of the war unless he revisited its horrors and shared them with others: 'I must go over the ground again ...' he wrote as his justification for producing *Undertones of War*. He admitted that 'there are many recollections to choose from, and who can say how any of us decides what exact path to take through the still richly remembered past?' Does this mixture of motives and emotions admitted by the author modify your response to the passage just quoted?

The context of writing: the remembered past and the imagined past

Reading, and writing about, the literature of the Great War today it is important to be as aware as Blunden was that each writer chooses his or her own path through the 'richly remembered' past. Is the same true when reading about the Great War as imagined (in fiction) by writers who were not even alive at the time? The context in which a text was written is one of the most important aspects you need to consider when writing about any text in the literature of the Great War.

Consider the following passage from Sebastian Faulks' novel *Birdsong* (1993):

Queues were drifting and forming outside a shop where an improvised bar, which they called an estaminet, had been set up. Using his gifts as master of revels, Jack lighted on a cottage with a bright kitchen and a small queue. The men followed him and waited until there was space for them to crowd round a table where an elderly woman produced plates full of fried potatoes from a pan of seething oil. There were litre bottles of unlabelled white wine passed around among the diners. The men disliked the dry taste of it and one of the younger women was prevailed on to fetch sugar which they stirred into their glasses. Still pantomiming their disgust, they managed to swallow it in quantity. Jack tried a bottle of beer. It was not like the beer memory served him in the Victorian pubs at home, made with Kentish hops and London water ... [He] told a series of jokes in the style of a music hall comic. The men joined in with some of the punchlines, but kept laughing at his performance. Jack's solemn face glistened with the effort of his comedy, and the men's determined response, whistling and slapping each other in mirth, was a token of their determination, and their fear.

▶ Compare this passage with the extracts from 'Madame of the Inn' and *Undertones of War*. What difference does it make that this passage is drawn from imagination not memory? In what senses, if any, can you apply the word 'authentic' to it? How important (or intrusive) is the narrator here? Look particularly at the style of writing: in what ways can you describe it as more or less 'literary' than that of Edmund Blunden?

In writing about the literature of the Great War and about the Great War in British literature you will often be comparing texts, and though these may range from short poems to full-length novels, the principles will be the same as for the three short extracts above. What type of texts are they? Who wrote them, for whom and when? In what ways can they be read today and how do they illuminate each other? What other texts or types of text might help to clarify their meaning and their significance within the genre of Great War literature?

Your own and other readers' interpretations

In writing about the Great War it is important to reach your own view of any text, and also to recognise that other readers may read that same text in different ways. In this sense your writing is both a dialogue with the text you are studying and a dialogue with other readers, whose views may or may not coincide with yours; in any event, they are likely to make you rethink or confirm your own.

▶ To illustrate this point, read the poem 'The Silent One' by Ivor Gurney (Part 3, page 80). After a first reading, note down your initial impressions:

- What is the point of calling the poem 'The Silent One'?

- How does the title affect the way you read the poem?

- What is the situation described by Gurney?

- What points is he making in the poem about language and the way people speak?

- How does the way the poem is written help to convey the speaker's attitude to life and death in the trenches?

Now consider the following comments on the poem by P.J. Kavanagh from his Introduction to *Collected Poems of Ivor Gurney* (1982):

> There is no mythologising of the dead boy on the wires – surely the most appalling and demoralising sight the troops on the Western Front had to endure – nor any attempt to shock. What is missed is his 'chatter': not loss of promise, ending of beauty and youth – grander conceptions which may come later – but the sudden cessation of the small inconsequences of life. That the chatter had the stamp of Buckinghamshire on it would have been as significant to the dead soldier as Gurney's Gloucestershire background was to him.
>   Then the poem, in a domestic fashion, goes on to describe how Gurney disobeyed an order, on the grounds of common sense, and apparently got away with it:
>
>> Till the politest voice – a finicking accent, said:
>> 'Do you think you might crawl through there: there's a hole'.
>> Darkness, shot at: I smiled, as politely replied –
>> 'I'm afraid not, Sir' ...
>
> 'Finicking' is precise, and the exchange of politenesses comic. Already, quickly moving, impressionistic, this is not quite like any war poem one has read.

How far do Kavanagh's comments here reinforce or modify your own impressions of the poem? His starting point is evidently one of sympathy for the horrors faced by men at the Front: he claims that Gurney presents the image of the corpse on the wire (note Kavanagh's own description of the soldier as 'the dead boy') without giving him any symbolic significance – 'there is no mythologising'. Do you accept the phrases 'in a domestic fashion' and 'the exchange of politenesses comic' as apt descriptions of Gurney's way of reporting the conversation with the commanding officer?

Now compare Kavanagh's comments with those of another critic, Martin Coyle:

> Gurney writes with bitter humour ... The officer asks the speaker to go through the wire, but his asking is a command. There is no hole, but the officer knows that; he's looking for a volunteer to get through or throw himself on it. The speaker replies that he cannot and so lives. The poem uses this dialogue to pinpoint a symbolic moment when language is turned on language to resist the tyranny of patrician [upper class] discourse.
>
> That tyranny is registered at the opening of the poem in the spectacle of the figure on the wire, hung like Christ on the cross, a figure who serves to highlight the source from which patrician authority takes its moral posturing. The class struggle that is being fought through the war exposes the patrician codes as shaped not just by social and political values but also by religious and linguistic ones. Under the guise of sacrifice for a greater good, the ruling class masters the troops into repeated sacrifice on the basis of how they speak. What is stressed about the now 'silent one' is his 'chatter and his Bucks accent', both of which offend the invisible rules of class which demand silent obedience. But not just of class. 'Chatter' carries with it connotations of the feminine – it is 'infinitely lovely' – so that surrounding the death of the Bucks ranker are anxieties about gender, anxieties about how his chattering undermines notions of masculine heroism.
>
> (Martin Coyle 'Language, Class, Death and Landscape'
> in *English* vol 44, part 179, 1995)

Unlike Kavanagh, Coyle is not concerned in this essay with the horrors experienced by men fighting the enemy across No Man's Land: he is focusing on the class war being waged between the officers and ordinary soldiers on the same side. Coyle does not accept that 'there is no mythologising of the dead boy on the wires'; he argues that this is a symbolic crucifixion – the soldier 'hung on the wire' as Jesus hung on the cross – and that the Christian symbolism here 'exposes the moral posturing' of the officer who claims the moral right to give an order which will almost certainly send a man of lower social and military rank to his death.

These two, very different, responses to Gurney's poem show how important it is to recognise that there may be other points of view apart from your own which need to be considered. They can also be challenged: is not Kavanagh himself mythologising the corpse on the wire by sentimentally depicting him as 'the dead boy' (innocent youth cruelly destroyed by modern war)? Do you find Coyle's claim (on which much of his argument depends) that the figure is hung 'like Christ on the cross' justified by the evidence of the poem itself? Do you find Kavanagh's 'comic' or Coyle's 'bitter humour' (or neither) an appropriate way to describe the tone and form of the poem?

These questions emphasise the final, but most fundamental point of all: when writing about the literature of the Great War and about the Great War in British literature, you must start and end with the texts themselves. In the end all the issues that you must deal with – writers' use of language, your own and other reader's interpretations, the contexts in which texts were written and understood – depend entirely on your dialogue with what the writers themselves have written.

Assignments

The following tasks and questions are designed to help you think, either as a member of a group or on your own, about the issues raised when studying the Great War in British literature (as a theme) and the literature of the Great War (as a genre). Some of them could involve extended research leading to a project; others may simply be the starting point for a discussion, or for your own thoughts and ideas to focus on a particular aspect of the subject.

Remember that literature is the written evidence of what matters most to the society which produces it. It both reflects and shapes the thinking and feeling of that society, so it is always important to bear in mind the cultural context in which a text was written and the contexts in which it was first read and can be read today. (Think about Isaac Rosenberg's poem 'Returning, We Hear the Larks' compared with Sebastian Faulks' novel *Birdsong*.)

1 Study the poems by Marian Allen (page 75) and the extracts from Vera Brittain (page 78), Irene Rathbone (page 87) and Rebecca West (page 95). How clear and consistent a sense do these texts give you of women's responses to the Great War?

2 Explore the way in which popular culture of the period (for example, songs, music hall entertainment, early cinema and newsreel film) influenced the work of writers of the Great War itself, or of later writers returning to the Great War as a subject.

3 During the Great War (as in subsequent wars) governments commissioned artists to record scenes of war and wartime life as a

national record. By researching the work of painters such as Paul Nash, Stanley Spencer or C.W. Nevinson, compare and contrast the way artists and writers have recorded the landscapes and activities of war.

4 War memorials are some of the most lasting and visible reminders of the Great War. Visit and describe some local memorials and then reread the poems about war memorials in Part 3 (for example, pages 86 and 92). Do you think the attitudes expressed in such poems – or in other writing from the 1920s and 1930s – are still appropriate today?

5 Why do you think the Great War continues to occupy a much more important role in British literature and culture than it does in the literature and culture of other countries?

6 War both sharpens and challenges preconceived idea about nationhood. A question asked explicitly in Shakespeare's *Henry V* (and implicitly in his other history plays) is 'What is my nation?' How is this question asked, and answered, in the literature of the Great War that you have studied?

7 There was a brief but strong revival of interest in Great War writing at the end of the 1920s and start of the 1930s. By comparing and contrasting some of the books published in this period (see Chronology, pages 118–120), suggest what might have led to this revival, and analyse the main attitudes to the war expressed in the books you have studied.

8 How did the Second World War affect the writers who had survived the First? How has it affected the way the literature of the Great War has been interpreted since 1945?

9 Select two or three anthologies of Great War literature (preferably published at different times during the 20th century) and review them to explore their scope and success in presenting a picture of the Great War. It is important to read their Introductions to judge how clearly the editors have set out their own views and ideas.

10 After reading as much as you can of the writing discussed in this book, how easy do you find it to distinguish between 'the war remembered' and 'the war imagined'?

6 | Resources

Chronology of texts and writers discussed

The dates given are those of first publication of each book.

1912   *Georgian Poetry 1* (first Georgian anthology)

1914   *Des Imagistes* (first Imagist anthology)

1915   *Georgian Poetry 2*; Rupert Brooke *1914 and Other Poems*

1916   Charles Sorley *Marlborough and Other Poems*; Robert Graves *Over the Brazier*; Henri Barbusse, *Le Feu* (*Under Fire* – novel)

1917   *Georgian Poetry 3*; Ivor Gurney *Severn and Somme*; Siegfried Sassoon *The Old Huntsman*; Robert Graves *Fairies and Fusiliers*; Edward Thomas Poems; John Drinkwater *x = o* (drama)

1918   Edward Thomas *Last Poems*; Rebecca West *The Return of the Soldier* (novel); Siegfried Sassoon *Counter-Attack*; Vera Brittain *Verses of a V.A.D.*

1919   *Georgian Poetry 4*; Richard Aldington *Images of War*; George Bernard Shaw *Heartbreak House* (drama)

1921   Ernest Raymond *Tell England* (novel); Virginia Woolf *Jacob's Room* (novel)

1922   *Georgian Poetry 5*; T.S. Eliot *The Waste Land*

1923   Richard Aldington *Exile and Other Poems*

1924   Ford Madox Ford *Parade's End* (1924–1928 – novel)

1925   Virginia Woolf *Mrs Dalloway* (novel)

1928   Edmund Blunden *Undertones of War*; Siegfried Sassoon *Memoirs of a Fox-hunting Man*; R.C. Sherriff *Journey's End* (drama)

1929   Robert Graves *Goodbye to All That*; Richard Aldington *Death of a Hero* (novel); Eric Maria Remarque *Im Westen Nichts Neues* (*All Quiet on the Western Front* – novel); Virginia Woolf *A Room of One's Own* (essay)

1930   Siegfried Sassoon *Memoirs of an Infantry Officer*; Richard Aldington *Roads to Glory* (short stories)

1931   Wilfred Owen *Collected Poems* (ed. Blunden)

1932   Irene Rathbone *We That Were Young* (novel)

1933   Vera Brittain *Testament of Youth* (autobiography); Herbert Read *The End of a War*

1937   Isaac Rosenberg *Complete Works*; Edmund Blunden *An Elegy* (contains 'Echoes from the Great War'); David Jones *In Parenthesis*

1941   Richard Aldington *Life for Life's Sake* (memoirs)

1945   Siegfried Sassoon *Siegfried's Journey* (memoirs)

1954   Ivor Gurney *Poems* (ed. Blunden)

1955   Robert Graves *Collected Poems*

1960   H.D. *Bid Me to Live* (novel)

1962   Benjamin Britten *War Requiem*

1964   Brian Gardner (ed.) *Up the Line To Death* (anthology)

1965   Ian Parsons (ed.) *Men Who March Away* (anthology)

1967   Joan Littlewood/Theatre Workshop *Oh, What a Lovely War!* (drama); Wilfred Owen *Letters*

1971   Susan Hill *Strange Meeting* (novel)

1974   Jon Stallworthy *Wilfred Owen* (biography)

1975   Joseph Cohen *Journey to the Trenches: the Life of Isaac Rosenberg*

1978   Michael Hurd *The Ordeal of Ivor Gurney* (biography)

1979   Jon Silkin (ed.) *The Penguin Book of First World War Poetry*

1981   Catherine Reilly *Scars Upon My Heart* (anthology)

1989   Charles Doyle *Richard Aldington* (biography)

1990   Barry Webb *Edmund Blunden* (biography)

1991   Pat Barker *Regeneration* (novel)

1993   Sebastian Faulks *Birdsong* (novel); Pat Barker *The Eye in the Door* (novel)

1995   Pat Barker *The Ghost Road* (novel)

1996   Edmund Blunden *Overtones of War* (poetry)

1998   Jean Moorcroft Wilson *Siegfried Sassoon* (biography); Mark Bishop & Alan Bostridge (eds.), *Letters of a Lost Generation* (letters from and to Vera Brittain)

1999   John Stuart Roberts *Siegfried Sassoon* (biography); Nigel Jones *Rupert Brooke: Life, Death and Myth* (biography)

Further reading

Books by and about individual authors are listed in the Chronology (see pages 118–120).

Anthologies

Although the anthologies by Brian Gardner, Ian Parsons and Jon Silkin (see pages 96–98) are still important, a number of more recent additions are valuable resources for studying the poetry of the Great War

Dominic Hibberd and John Onions (eds.) *Poetry of the Great War* (Macmillan, 1986)
Authoritative and comprehensive edition.

Robert Giddings (ed.) *The War Poets* (Bloomsbury, 1988)
Contains commentary, biographical notes and an excellent range of paintings and illustrations from 1914–18 to put the poetry into context.

Tim Cross *The Lost Voices of World War I* (Bloomsbury, 1988)
Both an anthology of prose and poetry from writers who were killed in the war and a valuable introduction to European (not just British) writing from the period. Contains a lucid introduction to modernism in the context of Great War poetry.

Martin Stephen (ed.) *Poems of the First World War* (Everyman, 1993)
A remarkably broad and broad-minded selection of material; refuses to take any received opinions for granted; very useful biographical notes and commentary.

Adrian Barlow (ed.) *Six Poets of the Great War* (Cambridge Literature, 1995)
Contains substantial selections of poetry by Edward Thomas, Isaac Rosenberg, Wilfred Owen, Siegfried Sassoon, Edmund Blunden and Richard Aldington, with notes and resource material.

Anne Powell (ed.) *The Fierce Light: The Battle of the Somme July – November 1916: Prose and Poetry* (Aberporth Palladour Books, 1996)
A unique anthology, tracing the course of the Battle of the Somme, almost day by day, through the letters, poems, diaries and memoirs of those who actually fought in it. Invaluable for examining the overlap between 'documentary' and 'literary' writing.

Critics

Bernard Bergonzi *Heroes' Twilight* (Constable, 1965);
Jon Silkin *Out of Battle* (OUP, 1972)
These remain the fullest surveys of British writing in the Great War.

Elizabeth A. Marsland *The Nation's Cause: English, French and German Poetry of the First World War* (Routledge, 1991)
A genuinely European survey of the poetry of the Great War, with a clear focus on the idea of nationhood and poetry as an expression of cultural identity.

Simon Featherstone *War Poetry: An introductory reader* (Routledge, 1995)
This is an important book, combining a thorough discussion of contemporary critical and cultural issues with an innovative anthology of poetry and prose commentary from both the First and Second World Wars.

Cultural studies

Paul Fussell *The Great War and Modern Memory* (OUP, 1975)
Samuel Hynes *A War Imagined: the First World War and English Culture* (Pimlico, 1992)
Samuel Hynes *The Soldiers' Tale: Bearing Witness to Modern War* (Pimlico, 1998)
The first two studies are the two most authoritative and wide-ranging discussions of the Great War in its cultural context. To these should now be added *The Soldier's Tale*, which contains chapters on the literature (documentary, literary and historical) of both World Wars and of the Vietnam War.

Jay Winter *Sites of Memory, Sites of Mourning* (Cambridge, 1995)
Aptly described as a study of the 'collective remembrance' of the Great War. Includes chapters on the apocalyptic imagination in literature and in art.

Allyson Booth *Postcards from the Trenches: Negotiating the Space between Modernism and the First World War* (OUP, 1996)
As its title implies, this book is both lively and serious, with particularly interesting discussions of the physical and aesthetic evidence of war and remembrance.

Trudi Tate *Modernism, History and the First World War* (Manchester University Press, 1998)
Applies a specifically feminist perspective to the literature, propaganda and machinery of the Great War; very interesting discussions on Aldington, H.D., D.H. Lawrence and Virginia Woolf.

Websites

The number and variety of websites dealing with the period is already bewildering. Two are essential for anyone interested in the literature of the Great War:

First World War and Poetry Links
http://info.ox.ac.uk/jtap

This indispensable site offers virtual seminars on the literature of the Great War, focusing on individual poems and introductions to text analysis, using manuscripts of Wilfred Owen's poetry, as well as providing links to other key sites. It includes the complete run of *The Hydra*, the magazine edited by Owen while he and Sassoon were at Craiglockhart Hospital in 1917, as well as biographies and bibliographies.

http://www.links2go.com/topic/World_War_1

This site is the gateway to the best available range of sites dealing with all aspects of the Great War. An example of its scope: it offers access to the first American anthology of war poetry, *A Treasury of War Poetry, 1917*, edited by George Herbert Clarke. The entries and omissions in this anthology are very revealing.

Glossary

Canon those texts which are regarded as an indispensable part of a literature, or of a genre or topic within that literature. Shakespeare, for instance, is central to the canon of English literature (i.e. of the English-speaking world) and of specifically British literature, then there is the canon of his plays and a canon of Shakespeare criticism, etc.

Diction the choice of words (lexis) adopted by a writer, usually applied to poetry. May refer to a characteristically 'poetic' vocabulary, but more often to the way the writer's choice and use of language helps to create the tone and 'voice' of the writing (e.g. 'colloquial', 'rhetorical', etc.) and therefore to establish the relationship between speaker and listener/reader.

Dymock poets closely associated with the Georgian movement, the Dymock poets (a recent term) were a group of young writers who, during 1914–15, lived and/or spent time around the village of Dymock on the Gloucestershire-Herefordshire border. Wilfred Gibson and Lascelles Abercrombie were at the centre of the group, which also included Edward Thomas, Robert Frost, Rupert Brooke and John Drinkwater. Ivor Gurney, though not part of the group, visited and admired them – especially Edward Thomas, whose writing influenced his.

Genre although genre is often used loosely to refer to prose, poetry and drama as the three main forms of literary writing, it has a more specific meaning. Types of writing such as the Gothic novel or war poetry can be described as genres, identifying a group of texts that share key features of form, theme or approach.

Georgian Poetry writing associated with the *Georgian Poetry* anthologies, edited by Edward Marsh between 1912–22. (Georgian = written during the reign of George V, who had become king in 1910.) A major influence in English poetry before and during the Great War, Rupert Brooke, Robert Graves, Siegfried Sassoon, Edmund Blunden, John Drinkwater and Isaac Rosenberg were all published in the anthologies. Regarded as parochial and lacking in technical or intellectual rigour by the modernist poets (e.g. Richard Aldington, Ezra Pound and T.S. Eliot) whose dominance in the 1920s overshadowed the Georgian movement.

Imagism a movement established by Ezra Pound in 1912; centred on young (at that time unknown) poets such as Richard Aldington, H.D. and F.S. Flint. Influenced by developments in modern French writing and by unfamiliar verse forms such as Japanese haiku. Emphasis on 'concentration' of diction, experimental verse forms, and sharp focus on unusual and striking imagery. Influenced the early writing of T.S. Eliot.

Lyric   usually a short poem, often formal in style but intimate in tone, though in the 20th century such generalised definitions of the form came under strain. Poems such as Sassoon's 'Everyone Sang' or Edward Thomas's 'The Sun Used to Shine' would be regarded as lyric (and lyrical – i.e. happy and/or wistful – in tone), but Owen's 'Strange Meeting' or Rosenberg's 'Dead Man's Dump' would not.

Modernism   the dominant movement of thought and art (literature, music, painting, architecture, etc.) in the earlier 20th century, and still influential at the end of it. Originally a reaction against established 19th century (Romantic/Victorian) forms and attitudes, it was experimental not conservative, international, intellectual and metropolitan not rural and romantic, responding to the impact of the new technological age. Writers such as D.H. Lawrence, Virginia Woolf and T.S. Eliot were at the centre of literary modernism in Britain during the Great War and the 1920s.

Narrative/narrator   literally the sequential telling of an event or story; in prose (especially fiction) and often in poetry, it is important to describe the narrative structure of a text (the way the story/argument/situation, etc. is organised and presented) and to identify the narrative voice and/or the narrative perspective being adopted. It is appropriate to speak of a narrator (who may or may not be the poet himself) in poems such as Owen's 'Dulce et Decorum Est' or 'As The Team's Head Brass' by Edward Thomas. Prose, diaries, letters, etc. may contain narrative; a novel will have a narrator or narrators, who may be one of the characters (or the hero/heroine) or the author.

Index

Acknowledgements

The author and publishers wish to thank the following for permission to use copyright material:

Mark Bostridge and Rebecca Williams, Literary Executors of the Estate of the author, for excerpts from Vera Brittain, *Testament of Youth*, and *Letters From a Lost Generation: First World War Letters of Vera Brittain and Four Friends*, eds. Alan Bishop and Mark Bostridge, Little Brown and Company (1998); Carcanet Press for an extract from Robert Graves, 'A Dead Boche' from *Collected Poems*; and Charlotte Mew, 'The Cenotaph' from *Collected Poems and Prose*; Rosica Colin Ltd on behalf of the Estate of the author for Richard Aldington, 'Picket', 'Living Sepulchres' and 'In Memory of Wilfred Owen' and extracts from 'Eumenides', 'Field Manoeuvres', 'Meditation' from *Complete Poems*, ed. Alan Wingate; and extracts from *Death of a Hero* and *Roads of Glory*; Samuel French Ltd on behalf of the Estate of the author for an extract from John Drinkwater, $x = o$ in *Collected Plays*; Faber and Faber Ltd for extracts from T.S. Eliot, *The Waste Land* from *Collected Poems* 1909–1962; Ted Hughes, 'Six Young Men' from *The Hawk in the Rain*; David Jones, *In Parenthesis*; and with Farrar, Straus and Giroux, LLC for Philip Larkin, 'MCMXIV' from *Collected Poems*. Copyright © 1988, 1989 by the Estate of Philip Larkin; David Higham Associates on behalf of the Estate of the author for Herbert Read, 'To a Conscript of 1940' from *World Within a War*, Faber and Faber (1944); P.J. Kavanagh for Ivor Gurney, 'The Silent One' and extracts from 'After War' and 'The Billet' from *Ivor Gurney: Selected Poems*, ed. P.J. Kavanagh, Oxford University Press (1980); Barbara Levy on behalf of George Sassoon for *Siegfried Sassoon*, 'Reconciliation', 'To One Who Was With Me in the War', 'On Passing the New Menin Gate', extracts from 'Glory of Women', 'The Hero', *Siegfried's Journey*, Faber and Faber (1945) and 'A Soldier's Declaration', included in Robert Graves, *Goodbye to All That*. Copyright © Siegfried Sassoon; The Mid Northumberland Arts Group for Ivor Gurney, 'To England – a Note' from *Severn and Somme*; Peter Newbolt for an extract from Henry Newbolt, 'Vitai Lampada' included in *Poems: New and Old* by Henry Newbolt, John Murray; Oxford University Press for extracts from Jon Stallworthy, *Wilfred Owen* (1974) pp. 285–286; and *Wilfred Owen: Collected Letters*, eds. Harold Owen and John Bell (1967); Penguin Books for extracts from Pat Barker, *The Ghost Road*, Viking (1995) pp. 272–273, 275. Copyright © Pat Barker 1995; The Peters Fraser and Dunlop Group Ltd on behalf of the Estate of the author for Edmund Blunden, 'To W.O. and His Kind', 'To Wilfred Owen' and an extract from 'Can You Remember?' from *Overtones of War*; Laurence Pollinger Ltd on behalf of the Estate of Frieda Lawrence Ravagli for D.H. Lawrence, 'With the Guns', *Manchester Guardian*, 18 August 1914; Princeton University Press for extracts from *Letters from Ford Madox Ford*, ed. Ernest Raymond (1968); Random House Group Ltd, with Kay Collyer & Boose LLP on behalf of the Estate of Lady Elizabeth Glendevon, for an extract from W. Somerset Maugham, *For Services Rendered*, William Heinemann (1953); and with Random House, Inc for extracts from Sebastian Faulks, *Birdsong*. Copyright © 1993 by Sebastian Faulks; Vernon Scannell for 'The Great War'; A.P. Watt Ltd on behalf of The National Trust for Places of Historic Interest or Natural Beauty for an extract from Rudyard Kipling, 'For All We Have and Are'.

Every effort has been made to reach copyright holders; the publishers would like to hear from anyone whose rights they have unknowingly infringed.